statues Arkansas. Laws

Digest of Laws Relating to Free Schools in the State of

Arkansas

For School Officers

statues Arkansas. Laws

Digest of Laws Relating to Free Schools in the State of Arkansas
For School Officers

ISBN/EAN: 9783744666954

Printed in Europe, USA, Canada, Australia, Japan

Cover: Foto ©Suzi / pixelio.de

More available books at **www.hansebooks.com**

DIGEST OF LAWS

RELATING TO

FREE SCHOOLS

IN THE

STATE OF ARKANSAS.

FORMS FOR USE OF SCHOOL OFFICERS.

PUBLISHED BY AUTHORITY.

LITTLE ROCK:
A. M. WOODRUFF, STATE PRINTER,
1885.

CHAPTER CXXXV

OF

MANSFIELD'S DIGEST.

FREE SCHOOLS—SUPPORT OF.

SECTION 6119. Intelligence and virtue being the safeguards of liberty, and the bulwark of a free and good government, the state shall ever maintain a general, suitable and efficient system of free schools, whereby all persons in the state, between the ages of six and twenty-one years, may receive gratuitous instruction.

SEC. 6120. The general assembly shall provide, by general laws, for the support of common schools by taxes, which shall never exceed in any one year two mills on the dollar on the taxable property of the state; and by an annual per capita tax of one dollar, to be assessed on every male inhabitant of this state over the age of twenty-one years. *Provided*, the general assembly may, by general law, authorize school districts to levy, by a vote of the qualified electors of such district, a tax not to exceed five mills on the dollar in any one year for school purposes. *Provided, further,* that no such tax shall be appropriated to any other purpose, nor to any other district, than that for which it was levied. *Art. XIV, secs.* 1 *and* 3, *Const.*

COMMON SCOOL FUND.

SEC. 6121. The proceeds of all lands that have been, or hereafter may be, granted by the United States to this state, and not otherwise appropriated by the United States or this state; also all moneys, stocks, bonds, lands and other property now belonging to any fund for purposes of education; also the net proceeds of all sales of lands and other property and effects that may accrue to this state by escheat, or from sales of estrays, or from unclaimed dividends, or distributive shares of the estates of deceased persons; also any proceeds of the sale of public lands which may have been, or may be hereafter, paid over to the state (congress consenting); also ten per cent. of the net proceeds of the sales of all state lands; also all the grants, gifts or devises that have been, or hereafter may be made to this state, and not otherwise appropriated by the tenure of the grant, gift, or devise, shall be securely invested and sacredly preserved as a public fund that shall be designated as the "common school fund" of the state, and which shall be the common property of the state, except the proceeds arising from the sale or lease of the sixteenth section (*).

SEC. 6122. The annual income from the said fund, together with one dollar per capita to be annually assessed on every male inhabitant over the age of twenty-one years, and so much of the ordinary annual revenues of the state as may hereafter be set apart by law for such purposes, shall be faithfully appropriated for maintaining a system of free common schools for this·

(*) No money or property belonging to the public school fund, or to this state, for the benefit of schools or universities, shall ever be used for any other than for the respective purposes to which it belongs. *Art. XIV, sec.* 2, *Const.*

state, and shall be appropriated to no other purpose whatsoever. *Act Dec.* 7, 1875, *secs.* 1 *and* 2.

-SEC. 6123. The state auditor shall on requisition from the state superintendent of public instruction, draw warrants on the state treasurer for payment to the several county treasurers of the school revenues due their respective counties.

SEC. 6124. The per capita tax levied by the general revenue laws of the state shall be collected by the county collector at the same time and place that the state taxes are collected, and be paid into the county treasury on or before the first day of July of each year, in the presence of the county court clerk, who shall make a record of the same as a revenue for the support of common schools (†). *Ib., secs* 31 *and* 32.

COLLECTION OF CLAIMS DUE THE COMMON SCHOOL FUND.

SEC. 6125. The late county common school commissioners in the several counties in this State, or other persons holding moneys, notes, bonds or other papers belonging to the common school fund, shall be and they are hereby required to turn over the same into the hands of the collectors of their respective counties when ordered to do so by the board of commissioners of the common school fund. *Act March* 13, 1869, *sec.* 1.

SEC. 6126. Before taking charge of any such moneys, bonds notes and other papers each collector shall be required to give bond for the faithful keeping and delivering of the same, in such sum, double the amount supposed to come into his hands, and with such security as shall be approved by the county court, which bond, when approved, shall be filed with the county clerk ; and for such service said collector shall receive one per cent. of the net amount of such claims, when collected, payable upon the order of the board of commissioners of the common school fund. *Ib., sec.* 2.

SEC. 6127. It shall be the duty of each collector to receipt to any ex-school commissioner or other person for such moneys,

(†) The penalty collected for the non-payment of taxes on personal property is to be paid into the county school fund. See SEC. 5746.

notes, bonds or other papers as he may receive from him, and
safely keep the same subject to the order of the board of commissioners of the common school fund, and he shall deliver them to
the prosecuting attorney of the judicial circuit in which he may
reside, or to such other officer or person as said board may direct.
Ib., sec. 3.

SEC. 6128.　Any collector who shall fail to deliver any moneys,·
bonds, notes or other papers belonging to the common school
fund, for ten days after receiving the proper order from the commissioners of the common school fund, or in any manner con-
vert to his own use said moneys, bonds, notes or papers, or any
portion of them, shall, on conviction thereof, be imprisoned in
the penitentiary not less than five nor more than ten years. *Ib.,
sec.* 4.

SEC. 6129.　Whenever the board of commissioners of the
common school fund shall order the collector to deliver any of
said moneys, notes, bonds or papers to any officer or person, they
shall furnish a copy of said order to such officer or person, who,
if he shall not receive from the collector such moneys, notes,
bonds or papers within the time specified in the foregoing section, shall present the fact to the grand jury at the next term of
the circuit court for the county in which such collector may reside, and, upon failure to do so, he shall be deemed guilty of a
misdemeanor, and shall be fined in a sum not less than one hundred nor more than five hundred dollars. *Ib., sec.* 5.

SEC. 6130.　If default be made in the regular payment of interest due upon money loaned, or for lands sold by any common
school commissioner or township treasurer, or in the payment of
the principal, interest at the rate of ten per cent. per annum
shall be charged upon the principal and interest from the day of
default, which shall be included in the assessment of damages,
or in the judgment, in suits or action brought upon the obliga-
tion to enforce payment thereof; and interest, as aforesaid, may
be recovered in actions brought to recover interest only. *Act
Jan.* 11, 1853, *sec.* 52.

SEC. 6131.　The board of commissioners of the common school

fund shall be and they are hereby empowered and authorized, when they deem it necessary and appropriate, to employ counsel other than the prosecuting attorney or attorney-general in the adjudication and collection of outstanding claims of the common school fund in the several counties of the state ; and such counsel, when so employed, shall be allowed a reasonable compensation for their services, not to exceed five per cent, of the amount in controversy, to be paid on the order of said board of commissioners; and a sufficient amount is hereby appropriated out of the common school fund for that purpose. *Provided*, no amount shall be paid for counsel to exceed five per cent. of the amount collected. *Act April* 12, 1869, *sec.* 3.

SEC. 6132. In the payment of debts by executors and administrators, the debts due the common school fund shall have a preference over all other debts, except funeral and other expenses attending the last sickness.

SEC. 6133. No justice of the peace, constable, clerk of a court or sheriff shall charge any costs in any suit where the collector or any other officer sues for the recovery of any money due to the common school fund, if the plaintiff in such cause is unsuccessful. *Act Jan.* 11, 1853, *sec.* 50 *and* 55.

COMMISSIONERS OF SCHOOL FUND.

SEC. 6134. The governor, secretary of state and state superintendent of public instruction shall constitute a board of commissioners of the common school fund, and shall meet semi-annually at the office of said superintendent on the first Monday in February and on the first Monday in August in each year. *Provided*, that the governor may assemble the members of said board any time, at his discretion.

SEC. 6135. The governor shall be president of said board, and shall sign the journal of each day's proceedings.

SEC. 6136. The superintendent of public instruction shall act as secretary of the said board, and shall keep a faithful, correct record of the proceedings, and shall keep the said record open at all times for inspection. A copy of said record, certified by the secretary of the board, shall be in all cases received as evidence equal with the original.

SEC. 6137. The said board of school commissioners shall have the management and investment of the common school fund belonging to the state, and shall, from time to time, as the same may accumulate, securly.invest the said funds in bonds of the United States or the State of Arkansas.

SEC. 6138. That all moneys required by law to be paid into the treasury, to the credit of the common school fund may, if the same be not paid within thirty days after they shall have become due and payable, be recovered, with interest due thereon, by action in any court having jurisdiction ; and such action shall be prosecuted by the attorney-general of the state, or by the prosecuting attorney of any judicial district within this state, when directed by the said board.

Sec. 6139. All moneys belonging or owing to the common school fund, as mentioned in section 6121, or accruing as revenues there from, together with the state school tax, shall be paid directly into the state treasury, and shall not be paid out except on the warrant of the auditor. *Act Dec.* 7, 1875, *secs.* 3–8.

SEC. 6140. The state auditor shall be the accountant of the said board, and shall, annually, on the first Monday in October, transmit to the governor and to the superintendent of public instruction a report of the condiction of the school fund on the first day of July last preceding, with an abstract of the accounts thereof in his office.

SEC. 6141. The auditor shall, under the direction of the board of commissioners, draw warrants on the state treasurer for the payment of all or any portion of the common school fund belonging to the state, for the purchase of bonds or other securities in which the same is by law invested.

SEC. 6142. The state treasurer shall, by virtue of such warrant, pay from the uninvested common school fund the purchase money for said securities, and shall receive and deposit the same in the state treasury for safe keeping, and receipt to the president of the board of commissioners for the kind and amount of such securities.

SEC. 6143. The said board shall, at their semi-annual meeting, settle with the state treasurer all accounts of the common school fund not before settled. *Ib., secs.* 9-12.

SUPERVISION OF PUBLIC SCHOOLS.

SEC. 6144. The supervision of public-schools, and the execution of the laws regulating the same, shall be vested in and confided to such officers as may be provided for by the general assembly. *Art. XIV, sec.* 4, *Cons.*

State Superintendent of Public Instruction.

SEC. 6145. At the next general election, and every two years thereafter, there shall be elected a state superintendent of public instruction, by the qualified electors of this state, as state officers are now elected.

SEC. 6146. Before entering upon the duties of his office, he shall take and subscribe the oath prescribed for officers by the constitution of this state, and shall file such oath with the secretary of state.

SEC. 6147. The superintendent of public instruction shall be charged with the general superintendence of the business relating to the free common schools of this state.

SEC. 6148. He shall open, at the seat of the state government (at the expense of the state), a suitable office, in which he shall keep all books, reports, documents and other papers pertaining to his department, and where he shall be in attendance when not necessarily absent on business, and have personal supervision of the business affairs of his office, and keep a clear and correct record thereof.

SEC. 6149. He shall furnish suitable questions for the examination of teachers to the county examiner; he shall hold a teachers institute annually in each judicial district of the state, to be called a normal district institute; he shall arrange the programme exercises for each of such institutes, and preside thereat. *Provided,* if he should not be present, the teachers who may have assembled may organize and hold such normal district institute.

SEC. 6150. He shall prepare and transmit to the county examiners school registers, blank certificates, reports and other printed

blanks, together with other suitable blanks, forms and printed instructions, to be forwarded to directors and other school officers, as
may be necessary to aid such officers in making their reports and
carrying into full effect the various provisions of the school law of
this state.

SEC. 6151. He shall exercise such supervision over the school
funds as to ascertain the amount and disposal made of the same,
their protection and safety when invested or deposited, and recommend measures for their security and preservation, and for rendering them most productive of revenues ; shall enforce the strict application of the school revenues to the legitimate purposes for which
they were intended, and shall, when directed by the commissioners
of the school fund, cause to be instituted, in the name of the State
of Arkansas, suits or action for the recovery of any portion of the
said funds or said revenues that may be squandered, illegally applied or unsafely deposited.

SEC. 6152. He shall, on or before the first day of November in
each year, prepare and submit to the governor of this state an annual
report, in writing, showing the number of persons between the ages
of six and twenty-one years residing in the state on the first day of
the preceding July ; the number of such persons in each county ; the
number of each sex ; the number of white; the number of colored ;
the whole number of such persons that attended the free common
schools of the state during the year ending the thirtieth day of the
last preceding June, and the number in each county that attended
during the same period ; the number of whites of each sex that attended, and the number of colored of each sex that attended the said
schools ; the number of common schools in the state ; the number of
pupils that studied each of the branches taught ; the average wages
paid teachers of each sex ; the relative average wages paid to male
and female teachers, respectively, according to the different grades
of their certificates; the number of school-houses erected during the
year, the material and cost thereof; the number previously erected,
the material of which they were constructed, their condition and
value ; the number with their grounds enclosed ; the counties in
which teachers' institutes were held, and the number that attended
the institutes in each county.

SEC. 6153. He shall likewise report the amount of permanent school fund belonging to the state at the close of the fiscal school year, and the amount of other property apportioned to school purposes ; the nature, kind and amount of such investments made of the same ; the safety and permanency of such investments; the amount of revenue accruing from the school funds; the income received from the per capita assessments of each county, and the amount derived from such assessment in all the counties of the state ; the income derived from all other sources, together with the amount derived from each ; likewise, in what sums, for what purposes and in what manner the said school revenue shall have been expended, and what amount of school moneys of various kinds are in the various county treasuries unexpended.

SEC. 6154. He shall include in his report such plans as he may have matured for the improvement of the common school system of this state; for the accumulation, the investment and the more judicious management of the common school fund, and, when he may deem it advisable, shall recommend measures for a more economical and advantageous collection and expenditure of the revenues accruing from the said fund ; and whenever it comes to his knowledge that any of the investments of the school funds are not safe, or that that any portion of the said fund is liable to be lost, that it is unproductive of revenue, or that any of the school revenues have been diverted from their proper channel or from the appropriate objects contemplated, he shall report the facts to the governor and to the general assembly, if in session.

SEC. 6155. He shall also append to his report a statistical table, compiled from the materials transmitted to his office by school officers, with proper summaries, averages and totals given.

SEC. 6156. He shall present such a comparison of results, and such an exhibit of his administration, and of the operation of the common free school system, together with such statements of the true condition of the schools of the state, as shall distinctly show the improvements and progress made from year to year in the department of public instruction.

SEC. 6157: The annual reports of the state superintendent to the governor shall be transmitted by the governor to the general assembly at the opening of the session.

SEC. 6158. He shall have his reports to the governor published as soon as practicable after they have .been made, and shall cause them to be distributed among the various school officers of the state, to be kept on file in their respective offices. *Provided*, he shall not have more than five thousand copies of such reports printed for any one year, the printing of such reports to be let out as other contracts for printing.

SEC. 6159. He shall, on the first Monday of July and on the first Monday of January of each year, make a *pro rata* apportionment to the several counties of the state of the remaining revenues in the state treasury, available for distribution for school purposes, on the basis of the number of persons between the ages of six and twenty-one years residing in the said counties, respectively, on the first Monday of July previous; and he shall publish a statement of the same, and as early as practicable shall transmit a copy thereof to each county examiner and to each of the several treasurers in the state, and to each county clerk, who shall submit the same to the county court at its next term; and he shall thereupon draw his requisition on the state auditor in favor of the treasurers of the several counties for such amounts as the said counties may be entitled to receive for the support of free common schools.

SEC. 6160. He shall, from time to time, publish in convenient pamphlet form, and furnish each school officer, the acts of the general assembly relating to common schools, and the decisions of the courts having competent jurisdiction in relation to the school laws; and he shall likewise, at the request of any school officer, render a decision relating to the intent, construction or administration of any portion of the school laws on which decisions shall not have been published, and he may, when he shall deem it advisable to have the opinion of the attorney-general, require said opinion to be given in writing.

SEC. 6161. He shall for the purpose of ascertaining the amounts, safety and preservation of the school funds, have access to the auditor's books and papers, with full power to use and inspect the same.

SEC. 6162. At the expiration of his term of office he shall deliver to his successor possession of his office, together with all books, records, documents, papers and other articles belonging or pertaining to his office.

SEC. 6163. He shall affix the seal of the department of public instruction to all official communications from his office.

SEC. 6164. Whenever a vacancy in the office of superintendent of public instruction shall occur, from death, resignation or otherwise, the governor shall appoint a person of suitable attainments to serve the remainder of the unexpired term. *Provided*, such vacancy shall occur within nine months from the next succeeding election; otherwise an election shall be ordered, as in case of state officers.

SEC. 6165. Neither the state superintendent nor county examiner shall act as agent for any author, publisher or bookseller, nor directly or indirectly receive any gift, emolument, reward or promise of reward for his influence in recommending or procuring the use of any book, school apparatus or furniture of any kind whatever, in any public school; and any school officer who shall violate the provisions of this section shall be deemed guilty of a misdemeanor, and subject to removal from office.

SEC. 6166. The state superintendent of public instruction shall have power to grant state certificates, which shall be valid for life, unless revoked, to any person in the state who shall pass a thorough examination in all those branches required for granting county certificates; and, also in algebra and geometry, physics, rhetoric, mental philosophy, history, Latin, the constitution of the United States and of the State of Arkansas, natural history and theory and art of teaching.

SEC. 6167. He shall prepare, for the benefit of the common schools of the state, a list of such text books on orthography, reading in English, mental and written arithmetic, penmanship, English grammar, modern geography and history of the United States, as are best adapted to the wants of the learner, and as have been prepared with reference to the most philosophical methods of teaching

those branches, and shall recommend the said text-books to teachers
and to directors throughout the state.

SEC. 6168.   He shall procure and adopt a seal for his office, and
furnish an impression and description of said seal to the secretary of
state, to be preserved in his office.   •

SEC. 6169.   A copy of any paper or document deposited or filed
in the office of superintendent of public instruction shall, when authenticated by the said seal, be evidence equal, to all intents and
purposes, with the original.

SEC. 6170.   The said superintendent shall prepare appropriate
forms for three several grades of certificates to be issued to teachers
by the county examiners.   He shall prepare suitable school registers,
in which teachers, at the close of the school term, are to make their
reports to the trustees of the name and age of each pupil, the date
of each pupil's entrance, the separate days on which each attended
school, the studies each pursued, the total attendance ; and shall
likewise prepare suitable forms for the reports of directors and
county examiners.   *Act. Dec* 7, 1875, *secs.* 13–30 *and* 33–37.

SCHOOL DISTRICTS.

SEC. 6171.   The boundaries of school districts in counties of this
State shall be and remain as now established, except that the county
court shall have power to alter the same whenever a majority of the
citizens residing therein shall petition the court so to do; but in all
changes due regard shall be had to the convenience of the citizens,
and all the territory in the county shall be embraced in said school
districts.

SEC. 6172.   Each school district shall be a body corporate, by
the name and style of "School District No.——, of the county
of——," and by such name may contract and be contracted with, sue
and be sued, in any of the courts of this State having competent
jurisdiction (‡).

SEC. 6173.   Every district shall hold in the corporate name of the
district the title of lands and other property which may be acquired

(‡) School districts are not liable for trespasses committed by their officers. *School District
No.* 11 *v. Williams*, 38—454.

S2

by said district for school district purposes. *Act Dec.* 7, 1875, *secs.* 39 *and* 53.

SEC. 6174.   No new school district shall be formed having less than thirty-five persons residing within the territory included in such new district of scholastic age, and no district now formed shall, by the formation of a new district, be reduced to less than thirty-five persons of scholastic age. *Act March* 11, 1881, *sec.* 6.

SEC. 6175.   The county court shall have the right to form new school districts, or change the boundaries thereof, upon a petition of a majority of all the electors residing upon the territory of the district to be so affected by such change within the territory to be included in the new district proposed. *Provided,* such territory have the requisite number of children and property to comply with the now existing laws in such cases provided. *Act March* 30, 1883, *sec.* 2.

APPORTIONMENT OF SCHOOL FUND.

SEC. 6176.   The county court, immediately on receiving notice of the distributive share of school revenue apportioned by the state superintendent to each county shall proceed to apportion to the several school districts of the county, in proportion to the number of persons between the ages of six and twenty-one years residing within the school district, respectively, on the first Monday of July previous, the said school revenue apportioned to the county, and shall forward to the county treasurer, and to each of the directors of each district, a statement of such apportionment, carefully distinguishing the sources from which the school revenues so apportioned are derived, and the amount due each school district in the county from each separate source, and shall see that the revenues from the public school fund are invariably paid to the county and to the school districts strictly in accordance with the apportionment made to them.

SEC. 6177.   Whenever a new district shall have been formed and organized, the court shall, at the next apportionment made thereafter, apportion to the new district school revenues in proportion to the number of persons between the ages of six and twenty-one years reported by the directors of the new district; *provided, always,* that the number of persons between the ages of six and twenty-one years reported in any year by the district directors of each county shall be taken as the quota of that county, and the number reported from each school district shall be taken as the quota of that district, and that the only basis on which an apportionment of the school revenue shall be made is to be the number of persons so reported each year by the district directors. *Act Dec.* 7, 1875, *secs.* 40, 41.

SEC. 6178. The county examiners of the several counties shall, annually, between the tenth and twentieth days of September, transmit, verified by affidavit, to the county clerks of their respective counties a written report, showing the number of persons between the ages of six and twenty-one years residing in each school district in their respective counties, as shown by the reports of the district directors made for the same year to the county examiners, as is now required by law.

SEC. 6179. The county clerks shall, during the first terms of their respective county courts held after the reception of the reports provided for in the preceding section, lay such reports before such county courts, to be used as a guide in making the apportionment of the general school fund to the various school districts. *Act March* 23, 1881.

SEC. 6180. Any county which, by a change of county lines, or by the formation of a new county or counties, shall fail to receive the school funds which justly should be apportioned to it, from the fact of its school population being reckoned with that of the county or counties to which the said funds may be apportioned, shall be re-imbursed for the loss thus incurred. Said loss shall be corrected in the first apportionment of the school revenue thereafter. *Provided*, that if such correction be not made in the first apportionment thereafter, it may be made in the second.

SEC. 6181. The amounts refunded according to the provisions of section 6180 shall be deducted from the funds apportioned to the counties which were the original recipients of the erroneously apportioned revenues.

SEC. 6182. Upon the presentation of the certificate of the superintendent of public instruction of the amount or amounts due any

county, by the provisions of this act, to the auditor, he shall draw
his warrant on the state treasurer for said amount or amounts in
favor of the treasurer of said county for the benefit of the school
fund, and in compliance with section 6180. *Act March 6, 1877.*

• COUNTY EXAMINERS.

SEC. 6183. The county court of each county shall, at the first
term thereof after each general election, appoint in each county not
divided into two judicial districts one county examiner, and in each
county divided into two judicial districts may appoint one county
examiner for each district, such examiner to be of high moral
character and schoolastic attainments ; and it shall be the duty of the
county clerk to issue a commission to the person so appointed, and
immediately to certify his name and post-office address to the superintendent of public instruction. *Act Dec. 7, 1875, sec. 42, as amended
by sec. 1, act March 20, 1883.*

SEC. 6184. Any appointments heretofore made by the county
courts for the districts of such counties as are mentioned in the preceding section in which an examiner has been appointed for each
district are hereby declared to be legal and valid appointments. *Act
March 20, 1883, sec. 2.*

SEC. 6185. Before entering upon the duties of that office, the
county examiner shall take and subscribe the oath prescribed for
officers by the constitution of this state, and file such oath in the
office of the county clerk.

SEC. 6186. It shall be the duty of such examiner to enamine
and license teachers of common schools; and he shall receive, as a
compensation for his services, the sum of two dollars for each examination, to be paid by the person applying for the same. He
shall hold, quarterly, at the county seat of each county, in a suitable
room to be provided by the county court, a public examination for
that purpose, and shall, previous to holding such examination, give
at least twenty days' notice thereof to the directors of each schive
district within the county, whose duty it shall be to file the original
notice in their office, and post, without delay, copies of said notice
in three or more of the most conspicious places within their district.

He shall conduct all examinations by written and oral questions and answers, but shall grant no certificates of qualification except in accordance with the provisions of law respecting teachers' certificates.

SEC. 6187. He shall at the time and places appointed for holding public examinations, examine, in orthography, reading, penmanship, mental and written arithmetic, English grammar, modern geography, history of the United States, all persons present and applying for an examination, with the intention of teaching; and if convinced that such persons are of good moral character, and are competent to teach successfully the foregoing branches, he shall give such persons certificates ranking in grades to correspond with the relative qualifications of the applicants, according to the standard adopted; but he shall not license any person to teach who is given to profanity, drunkenness, gambling, licentiousness or other demoralizing vices, or who does not believe in the existence of a Supreme Being; nor shall he be required to grant private examinations. He may cite to re-examination any person holding a license and under contract to teach any free school within his county, and on being satisfied, by a re-examination or by other means, that such person does not sustain a good moral character, or that he has not sufficient learning and ability to render him a competent teacher, he may, for these and other adequate causes, revoke the license of such person; and, in case of such revocation, he shall immediately give notice thereof to such teacher and the directors, and thereby terminate the contract between the said parties; but the wages of such teacher shall be paid for the time he shall have actually taught, prior to the day on which he received notice of the revocation of his license.

SEC. 6188. He shall issue three grades of certificates, to be styled, respectively, certificates of the first, and of the second, and of the third grades. Certificates of the first grade shall be valid, in the county for which they were issued, for two years. Those of the second grade shall be valid, in the county for which they were issued, for one year. Those of the third grade shall be valid, in the county, six months. But he shall not renew any certificate or grant a license without an examination of the applicant with reference thereto.

SEC. 6189. He shall keep a record of the age, name, sex, post-office address and nativity of each person licensed by him to teach, and of the date and grade of his certificate, and shall include such record in his report to the state superintendent.

SEC. 6190. He shall encourge the inhabitants to form and organize school districts, to establish public schools therein, under qualified teachers, to furnish suitable text-books for their children, and to send them to school. He shall direct the attention of teachers and school patrons to those methods of instruction that will best promote mental and moral culture, and to the most feasible and improved plan for building and ventilating school-houses. He shall labor to create among the people an interest in the public schools, and shall take advantage of public occasions, such as the dedication of school-houses, public examinations and institutes, to impress people with the importance of educating every child, and consequently of the duty of maintaining a system of free schools established by law. He shall receive the reports of the directors, transmit an abstract of the same to the state superintendent, and transmit therewith a report of the condition and prospects of the schools under his superintendence, together with such other information and suggestions as he may deem proper to communicate.

SEC. 6191. He shall annually, on or before the twentieth of September, prepare in tabular form an abstract of the reports made to him by the directors of the school districts embraced within his county, showing the number of organized districts in his county at the commencement of the year, on the first day of July preceding, the districts that have made their annual reports, the number of persons in each district between the ages of six and twenty-one years, distinguishing the sex and also the color of said persons; the number of said persons that attended school during the year; the average number of males and of females of each color in daily attendance; and the number that pursued each of the studies designated to be taught in the common schools; the number of teachers of each sex, employed in his county; the average wages paid per month to teachers of each sex, according to the grade of their certificate; the whole amount paid as teachers' wages in his county; the number of pupils that studied in his county, and the several branches taught; the number of school houses erected during the year in his county, material and cost of the same; the number before erected, the material used in their construction, their condition and value; the grounds of how many inclosed; the amount of money raised by tax in each district, for what purpose raised; the amounts that have been expended, and for what purposes, the amount of revenue received by his county from the common school fund, and received for the support of schools from each of all other sources; for what purposes and in what sums the said revenues were expended, and what amounts unexpended were, at the close of the school year, in the county treasury; and shall report also the number of deaf-mutes, blind and insane in each school district in his county, under thirty years of age, their names and their post-office.

SEC. 6192. He shall number the several school districts in his county in regular order from number one upward, and shall keep in his office a record and description of each district, with the boundaries clearly defined, and also a record of such changes or alterations in the boundaries of each as shall from time to time be made.

SEC. 6193. He shall have power to appoint some suitable person to hold teachers' institutes and examine teachers in his county, in case of his inability to attend such institutes and examinations.

SEC. 6194. The now acting county superintendents shall, immediately after the county courts shall have appointed the county examiners, deliver to said examiners all books, papers, records and other property now in their possession by virtue of their offices belonging to the state, and shall take receipts for the same; and the office of county superintendent is hereby abolished. *Act Dec. 7, 1875, secs. 43-52.*

SEC: 6195. If any county examiner shall be found incompetent, or shall be frequently neglectful of his duty, upon satisfactory proof, the county judge shall remove him from office and shall immediately appoint his successor. *Act March 11, 1881, sec. 7.*

SEC. 6196. If any county examiner shall neglect, fail or refuse to perform any of the duties required of him in section 6191, and shall not forward the abstract mentioned in said section to the superintendent of public instruction on or before the twentieth day of September of each year, he shall forfeit to the county the sum of twenty-five dollars, to be recovered as in this act provided, together with all costs, and be paid into the county treasury.' *Act March* 11, 1881, *sec.* 11.

ANNUAL SCHOOL MEETING.

SEC. 6197. The electors of each organized school district in this state shall annually, on the third Saturday in May, at two o'clock P. M., hold a public meeting, to be designated " The annual school meeting of the district." *Act Dec.* 7, 1875, *sec. 54, as amended by act March* 11, 1881.

SEC. 6198. All persons qualified to vote for county and state officers at the general election shall be deemed qualified electors of the school district in which they reside, and shall have the privilege of voting at all school meetings. ·

SEC. 6199. The electors of every school district shall, when lawfully assembled in annual district school meeting, with not less than five electors present, have the power, by a majority of the votes cast at such meeting, first to choose a chairman; second, to adjourn from time to time ; third, to appoint, when necessary, in the absence of the directors of the district, a clerk *pro tem.;* fourth, to elect a director for the district for the next three school years, who can read and write ; fifth, to designate a site for a school-house ; sixth, to determine the length of time during which a school shall be taught more than three months in a year; seventh, to determine what amount of money shall be raised by tax on the taxable property of the district sufficient, with the public school revenues apportioned to the district, to defray the expenses of a school for three months, or for any greater length of time they may decide to have a school taught during the year; *provided,* that no tax for purposes aforesaid greater than one-half of one per cent. on the assessed value of the taxable property of the district shall be levied;

and provided, further, that they may, if sufficient revenue can not be raised to sustain a school for three months in any one year, determine by ballot that no school shall be taught during such year, in which case the revenue belonging to such district shall remain in the treasury to the credit of such school district; eighth, to repeal and modify their proceedings from time to time.

SEC. 6200. The annual district election shall be held by the school directors as judges, who shall have power to appoint two clerks; and if any of the directors should not attend, the assembled voters may choose judges in the place of those not attending, and the judges and clerks shall take the oath prescribed by the general election law.

SEC. 6201. The ballot of the voter shall, in addition to the name of the persons voted for as directors, have written or printed on it the words "for tax," or "against tax," and also the amount of tax the voter desires levied.

SEC. 6202. When the polls are closed (*), the judges shall proceed to count the votes, ascertain the result and make return thereof to the county court, showing the number of votes cast for each person voted for school director, also the number cast for and against tax, and the number of votes cast for each amount or rate of tax voted for (a); such return, together with the ballots, shall be sealed up and delivered by one of the judges to the county clerk, at least ten days before the meeting of the county court for levying taxes.

SEC. 6203. The county court, at its said meeting for levying taxes, shall open the return and ascertain whether a majority of the votes cast be for tax; and if a tax has been voted, then the court shall determine the amount of taxes voted by taking the largest amount or rate of taxation voted for by a majority of the voters, which shall be levied and collected by the district so

---

(*) As to time for opening and closing the polls, see *Holland v. Davies'* 36—446.

(a) Unless the judges make return of the election or vote to the county court, it can not levy the tax. *Hodgkin v. Fry*, 33—716. The omission of the judges to state in their return the number of votes cast for and against the proposed tax will not defeat a levy adopted by the meeting. *Holland v. Davies*, 36—416. As to other irregularities, see same case and *Rogers v. Kerr*, 42--100,

voting; and if no rate shall have received such majority, then all the votes cast for the highest rate shall be counted for the next highest, and so on, till some rate voted shall receive a majority of all the votes cast. In other respects the election shall be held according to the general election law. *Act Dec.* 7, 1875, *secs. 55 and 56.*

SEC. 6204. All taxes voted for school purposes by any school district shall be levied by the county court at the same time the county taxes are levied, and shall be collected in the same manner as the county taxes are collected, at the same time and by the same person, and be paid into the county treasury, there to be kept subject to disbursement on the warrant of the school directors; *provided,* that no tax for the purposes aforesaid greater than one-half of one per cent. on the assessed value of the taxable property of the district shall be levied, which shall be done by ballot (aa). *Act Dec.* 7, 1875, *sec. 41.*

SCHOOL DIRECTORS.

SEC. 6205. At the annual school meeting, held on the third Saturday in May, there shall be elected, by the legal voters in each school district, a director, who shall hold his office for the term of three years from October fifteenth next ensuing, and until his successor shall have been elected and have qualified. *Provided,* that at the first annual school meeting of the district after the passage of this act, three school directors shall be elected, to hold office one, two and three years, respectively; *and provided, further,* that when a new school district shall have been formed under the provisions of this act, three directors shall be immediately elected by the electors of the new district, and shall hold their office for one, two and three years, respectively, and until their successors are elected and qualified as herein provided for. *Act Dec.* 7, 1875, *sec. 57, as amended by act March* 11, 1881, *sec. 2.*

(aa) The county court has no power to levy a school tax independent of action on the part of the electors of each school district for which the tax is levied; it can only cause to be placed on the tax books and collected such rates as are reported from the districts. An excessive levy vitiates the whole tax. *Worthen v. Badgett,* 32—496. See *Cairo & Fulton R. R. Co. v. Parks, Ib.,* 131; *Rogers v. Kerr,* 42—100.

Sec. 6206. Any person elected and accepting the position of director of a school district shall, within ten days after having been notified of his election, file his acceptance with his predecessor at the time in office, and shall, within ten days after the fifteenth of October, take and subscribe, before a justice of the peace or other competent officer, the oath prescribed for officers by the constitution of this state, and shall file the said oath in the office of the clerk of the county in which he resides. *Act Dec. 7, 1875, sec. 58.*

Sec. 6207. An old director shall, upon application of an incoming director, administer to him the oath of office. *Act March 11, 1881, sec. 5.*

Sec. 6208. Any person who shall have been elected or appointed a director, and shall neglect or refuse to qualify and serve as such, shall forfeit to his district the sum of ten dollars, which may be recovered by action against him at the instance of any elector in the district, and which, when collected, shall be paid into the county treasury by the officer before whom the action was maintained, and added, by the treasurer, to the school fund revenues appropriated to the district.

Sec. 6209. Any director who shall neglect or fail to perform any duties of his office shall forfeit to his district the sum of twenty-five dollars, to be recovered as directed in the preceding section, and to add in like manner to the school fund revenues apportioned to his district.

Sec. 6210. If the office of any director in a district becomes vacant, the electors of said district shall, in a district meeting assembled, within fifteen days after the occurrence of such vacancy, elect a director to serve the remainder of the unexpired term ; but if the district in which such vacancy occurs neglect or fail to elect a director to fill such vacancy, then the county court shall appoint from the electors of said district a director to serve the remainder of the term.

Sec. 6211. The trustees of the several school districts in each county in the state shall hold office and perform the duties required of boards of directors in this act until their successors are elected and qualified in regular manner, according to the provisions of this act.

Sec. 6212. The said board shall make provision for establishing separate schools for white and colored children and youths, and shall adopt such other measures as they may judge expedient for carrying the free school system into effectual and uniform operation throughout the state, and providing, as nearly as possible, for the education of every youth.

Sec. 6213. The directors shall have charge of the school affairs and of the school educational interests of their districts, and shall have the care and custody of the school-houses and grounds, the books, records, papers and other property belonging to the district, and shall carefully preserve the same, preventing waste and damage; and shall purchase or lease, in the corporate name of the district, such school-house site as may be designated by a majority of the legal voters at the district meeting; shall hire, purchase or build a school-house with funds provided by the district for that purpose; and may sell or exchange such site or school-house, when so directed by a majority of the electors of any legal meeting of the district.

Sec. 6214. They shall hire, for and in the name of the district, such teachers as have been licensed according to law, and shall make with such teachers a written contract, specifying the time for which the teacher is to be employed, the wages to be paid per month, and any other agreement entered into by the contracting parties, and shall furnish the teachers with a duplicate of such contract, and keep the original; and they shall employ no person to teach in any common school of their district unless such person shall hold, at the time of commencing his school, a certificate and license to teach, granted by the county examiner or state superintendent.

Sec. 6215. The term "month," wherever it occurs in any section of this act, shall be construed to mean twenty days, or four weeks of five days each. *Act Dec. 7, 1875, secs. 58-62.*

Sec. 6216. The directors of each school district in this state shall adopt and cause to be used in the public schools, in their respective districts, one series of text-books in each branch or science taught in the public schools of their respective districts, and no change in these books shall be made for a period of three years, unless it be by a petition of a majority of the voters of the district desiring the change. *Act March* 11, 1881, *sec.* 2.

SEC. 6217. They shall procure from the county examiner, and furnish the teacher at the commencement of the term, a register for his school, and require the said teacher to report, in the said register, at the close of the school term, the number of days of the said term, the name and age of each pupil, the date on which each entered the school, the separate days on which each attended, the whole number of days each attended, the studies each pursued, the total number of days all pupils attended, the average daily attendance and the number of visits received from the directors during the said term. *Act Dec.* 7, 1875, *sec.* 63.

SEC. 6218. They shall visit the schools at least once each term, and encourage the pupils in their studies, and give such advice to the teacher as may be for the benefit of teacher and pupils.

SEC. 6219. They shall submit to the district, at the annual meeting, an estimate of the expenses of the district for that year, including the expenses of a school for the term of three months for the next year, after deducting the probable amount of school moneys to be apportioned to the district for that school year, and shall also submit an estimate of the expenses per month of continuing the school beyond the term of three months, and of whatever else may be necessary for the comfort and advancement of the said school.

SEC. 6220. They shall, in all suits and action at law brought by or against their district, appear for and in behalf of said district. *Provided,* that they shall have no other directions or instructions by a lawful meeting of the electors of their district.

SEC. 6221. They shall draw orders on the treasurer of the county for the payment of wages due teachers, or for any lawful purpose, and they shall state in every such order the services or consideration for which the order is drawn, and the name of the person rendering such service; but they shall not draw any order on the county treasurer for the payment of the wages of any teacher not licensed.

SEC. 6222. When the warrant of any board of directors, properly drawn, is presented to the treasurer of the proper county, he shall pay the same out of any funds in his hands for that purpose belonging to the district specified in said warrant.

SEC. 6223. The directors shall give notice of each annual meeting, by posting notices thereof, at least fifteen days previous to such meeting, in three or more conspicuous places within the district (b) ; but it shall not be lawful for a district, at any annual meeting, to fix a site for a school-house, or to raise money for building or purchasing a school-house, unless the directors shall have particularly set forth in the previous notice given of such meeting that these matters were to be submitted for their consideration and action.

SEC. 6224. One of the directors shall act as clerk at all district meetings, shall keep a record of the proceedings thereof in a book provided for that purpose, or, if absent, shall transcribe into said book the minutes kept by the clerk *pro tempore*, and signed by the chairman, as so much of the authenticated records of the district ; and he shall enter on the said book copies of all his reports to the county clerk and the county examiner.

SEC. 6225. He shall keep, in a book provided for that purpose, the accounts of the district, by debits and credits, including the accounts with the county treasurer, and shall present the same to each annual meeting, showing the current expenses for the year, for school-houses, out-buildings, fences with which to inclose a school-house site, for stoves, wood, maps, charts, blackboards, a dictionary, and other necessaries for a school, and stating the number of days the directors have been necessarily employed in the performance of their duties as directors; the

---

(b) It is the duty of the directors to designate the place of the annual meeting, and notice of the time and place is essential to the validity of a tax voted at such meeting. But the statute designates the time, and all are bound to take notice of it. If notice of the place be given, the meeting will be legal, though the *time* be not specified in the notice. *Hodgkin v. Fry*, 33--716. A notice given by *two* of the directors is sufficient. *Holland v. Davies*, 36--446.

date of each order drawn by them on the county treasurer, and for what services or consideration, for what amounts and in whose favor, exhibiting vouchers therefor; a statement of the indebtedness of the district, and also of the surplus moneys, if any, in the county treasury belonging to the district at the commencement of the year; the amount of taxes levied on the district for school purposes within the year; the different purposes for which said taxes were levied, and the amount levied for each purpose. If, on examination, the report be found correct, the chairman of the meeting shall approve the same, and order that it be filed with the records of the district.

SEC. 6226. The directors shall, within ten days after any school meeting, report to the clerk of the county so much of the proceedings of said meeting as pertains to the election of officers; and they shall, on or before the first day of October in each year, furnish to the clerk so much of the copy of their record, attested by the chairman of the meeting, as shows the amount of money voted to be raised by the district, for school purposes, at the annual meeting.

SEC. 6227. They shall, annually, between the first and tenth days of September, transmit, verified by their affidavit, to the county examiner, a written report, in proper form, of the name of their county; of the number of their district; the names and ages of all persons, between the ages of six and twenty-one years, residing in their district on the first day of September; the number of males and females, respectively, of each color, that attended the common schools during the last school year; the average number of each sex that attended daily; the number that pursued each of the studies designated to be taught in the common schools of this state; the number of times the school was visited each term by the directors; the number of days that school was taught during the year by a licensed teacher; the name of each teacher; the grade of his certificate; the wages paid each teacher per month, and the whole amount of wages paid teachers during the year. They shall include in their report the amount of taxes voted by the district during the last school year, for what purpose voted, and the amount voted for each purpose; the amount drawn from the county treasurer for each purpose for which money was raised by district tax the previous year; the amount of revenues received from the common school fund, and the amount received from each of the various other sources from which school revenues are derived; the amount of each kind of revenue remaining in the county treasury and subject to the order of the district; the number of school-houses erected during the year, and the cost and material of each; the number, the material, the condition and value of those before erected, and the value of all other property belonging to the district; the condition of the school-house grounds, and whether the said grounds are inclosed; also, name, age and post-office of deaf, dumb, blind and insane in each district, including all who are blind or deaf to such an extent as not to be educated in common schools; and they shall record the said report in the proper place in the district book in which the current record of the proceedings of the district is kept.

SEC. 6228. If the directors of any district fail or neglect to make a report of the enumeration, statistics and finances of their district at the time and in the manner prescribed in the preceding section, the said directors, in addition to their forfeiture for neglect of duty, shall severally be liable for any damages, including the costs of the suit, that the district may sustain by reason of losing the school revenues that would otherwise have been apportioned to them.

SEC. 6229. They shall at the close of the school year, settle with the county treasurer, and ascertain what moneys, if any, to which their district may be entitled, and the amounts, severally, thereof that are in the county treasury and subject to be drawn by their district. *Ib., secs.* 64–75.

SEC. 6230. The directors of any school district may, at the instance of the teacher, suspend from the school any pupil for gross immorality, refractory conduct or insubordination, or for infectious disease. *Provided,* that such suspension shall not extend beyond the current term.

SEC. 6231. They may permit older persons to attend the school under such regulations as they may deem proper.

SEC. 6232. The county court shall have power, upon the petition of any person residing in a particular school district, to transfer the child, children or wards of such person, for educational purposes, to an adjoining district in the same county, or to an adjoining district in an adjoining county, and shall at once notify the county examiner of the county or counties and the directors of both districts.

Sec. 6233. The directors of the district to which such children have been transferred, at the time of taking the enumeration, shall include such children in the district to which they have been transferred, and they shall not be enumerated in the district where they reside. The district school tax of such person shall be added to the school revenues of the district to which he has been transferred, and shall not be included in the school revenues of the district where he resides.

Sec. 6234. Any person who transfers his child, children or wards and property to any district, for educational purposes, shall have the same right to vote in said district for directors and tax as other electors have of the district to which he is so transferred. Where such person is transferred to a district out of his county, the county treasurer of the county, wherein he resides, shall open an account with the district to which he is transferred, and his school taxes shall be credited to the same and paid on the warrants of the directors of the district to which he is transferred. *Provided, further,* any person transferring his property and children to an adjoining school district, for educational purposes, shall not have the right to vote for directors or tax out of his county, and to vote only in the political township in which he resides. *Ib., sec.* 76, *as amended by act March* 30, 1883, *sec.* 1.

Sec. 6235. The directors may permit a private school to be taught in the district school-house during such time as the said house is not occupied by a public school, unless they be otherwise directed by a majority of the legal voters of the district.

Sec. 6236. They shall cause the public schools in their district to be closed on the days appointed for public examination of teachers in their county, and also cause the said school to be closed during the session of the teachers' institute.

Sec. 6237. Directors and county examiners shall be exempt

from working on roads and public highways, and from serving on juries, during their term of office. *Ib., secs.* 77–79.

SEC. 6238. Any director or other person whose duty it may become to report to the county court the per cent. of tax levied by any school district at an annual meeting, and who shall neglect or refuse to do so in the manner and at the time provided by law, shall be liable for all loss which may be sustained by such failure and for all costs, and shall be fined not less than ten nor more than fifty dollars.

SEC. 6239. Within fifteen days after any special tax shall be voted by a school district at an annual meeting, it shall be the duty of the directors to furnish the county clerk with a certified list of all persons owning property in the district liable to pay such special tax.

SEC. 6240. Any person whose duty it is to execute sections 6216, 6239 or 6254, and who shall fail to do so, shall be fined not less than ten nor more than fifty dollars, and the same shall be paid into the county treasury. *Act March* 11, 1881, *sees.* 1, 3 *and* 9.

TEACHERS.

SEC. 6241. Any person who shall teach in a common school in this state, without a certificate of his qualification and his license to teach, shall not be entitled to receive for such services any compensation from revenues raised by tax or in anywise appropriated for the support of common schools ; *provided,* that if his license expire by limitation during any school, such expiration shall not have the effect to interrupt his school, or to debar his claim against school revenues for the payment of teachers' wages.

SEC. 6242. Every teacher shall keep a daily register of his school in the manner prescribed by law, and indicated by the blank school register to be furnished by the director at the commencement of his school.

SEC. 6243. It shall be the duty of each and every teacher to attend the public examination for teachers, to become members and attend the regular session of the teachers' institute as soon as the same shall have been established; and no teacher, when attending examination or the institute, shall be charged for loss of time while necessarily absent from his school to attend such examination or institute.

SEC. 6244. No teacher employed in any of the common schools shall permit sectarian books to be used as a reading or text-book in the school under his care.

SEC. 6245. Any teacher who shall have complied with the provisions of this act shall be paid from the first money received into the county treasury to the credit of the district; and his claim shall not be superseded by any subsequent claim (†); and no money in the county treasury belonging to any district shall, so long as there is any such claim filed against the said district, be applied to any purposes whatever other than the payment of teachers' wages. *Act Dec.* 7, 1875, *secs.* 80–84.

SEC. 6246. No teacher shall be entitled to the last month's pay for any school taught by him until he shall have returned to the directors of the district in which such school was taught the daily register furnished him, with all statistical work which teachers are by law required to perform, perfected and complete and no director shall otherwise issue an order for such last month's pay. *Act March* 11, 1881, *sec.* 4.

TRESPASS ON SCHOOL-HOUSES, ETC.

SEC. 6247. Any person who shall willfully destroy or injure any building used as a school-house, or for other educational purposes, or any furniture, fixtures or apparatus thereto belonging, or who shall deface, mar or disfigure any such building, furniture or fixtures, by writing, cutting, painting or pasting thereon any likeness, figure, words, or device, without the consent of the teacher or other person having control of such house, furniture or fixtures, shall be fined in a sum double the value of any such building, furniture, fixtures or apparatus so destroyed, and shall be fined in a sum not less than ten nor more

(†) See SEC. 6251.

than fifty dollars for each offense for writing, painting, cutting
or pasting in any such building, furniture or fixtures any such
words, figures, likeness or device, to be recovered by civil action
in any court of competent jurisdiction; and the punishment
provided in this section is in addition to, and not in lieu of, the
punishment provided by the statutes for such offenses (*). *Act
Dec. 7, 1875, sec. 86.*

SCHOOL WARRANTS—DISBURSEMENT OF FUNDS, ETC.

SEC. 6248. It shall be unlawful for county collectors and treasurers to purchase, or otherwise be the owners of or interested, directly or indirectly, in, any school warrant issued by any school
director of the county in which they reside.

SEC. 6249. The district school tax in each county may be payable and receivable in the warrants drawn by the directors of the
school district in which a school tax may be levied by the county
court.

SEC. 6250. It shall be the duty of the county treasurer of each
county to keep in his office a suitable and well-bound book, in
which he shall register by number and in the order of presentation
all district school warrants that may be presented to him; this regis-
tration to be made before the warrant is paid, and it shall show the
date of the presentation of the warrant, by whom drawn, on what
district, and in whose favor, and for what purpose drawn, the
amount and date of the warrant, date of payment, and to whom
paid; and said book shall at all times be subject to the inspection of
any tax-payer.

SEC. 6251. It shall be the duty of the county treasurers, immediately upon the receipt by them of any school funds, to give notice
of the amount and kinds of funds received, and from what sources
received, by written or printed notices put up in two public places
in each and every school district and at the court-house door, and
the funds so received shall be paid out *pro rata* on the warrants
registered in accordance with the provisions of the preceding section (†); *provided*, that application for such payment is made within
thirty days from the giving of the notice herein required.

(*) For an offense committed by insulting a teacher in the presence of his pupils, see SEC. 1807.
(†) See SEC. 6176.

Sec. 6252. Any officer failing to comply with the reqirements of this act, for each and every offense, shall be subject to indictment, and, if found guilty, shall be punished by a fine of not less than five hundred dollars and by confinement in the penitentiary of the state for a period not less than three nor more than twelve months.

Sec. 6253. Any director who shall fraudulently issue any school warrant shall be guilty of a misdemeanor, and, upon conviction, s hall be subject to the penalties enumerated in the preceding section. *Act May 27, 1874.*

Sec. 6254. The county treasurer shall, on or before the first day of September each year, forward to the superintendent of public instruction a certified statement showing the amount, in kind, of public school funds received by him; from what sources they were received; how and for what purposes they have been disbursed, and what amount, in kind, remains in the treasury. *Act March 11, 1881, sec. 8.*

Sec. 6255. The order of any board of directors, properly drawn after the passage of this act, other than those of single school districts in cities and towns, shall be presented to the treasurer of the proper county within sixty days after it was drawn by said board of directors. *Provided,* that if such order is not presented within the above specified time, it shall be rejected and become null and void. All such orders shall be paid in the order of their presentation.

Sec. 6256. If there are no funds with which to pay such order, the treasurer shall endorse the same, "Not paid for want of funds," giving the date and signing his name officially. Within thirty days thereafter, the holder of such order shall present it to the county clerk, who shall issue to him a warrant for the amount of such order at par, payable only at the county treasurer's office, when in funds to the credit of said district. He shall number and record each warrant in the book provided for such purpose, keeping a separate record for each district. *Provided,* that if such order is not presented within the above specified time, it shall be rejected and be null and void (bb). *Act Nov. 30, 1875, sec. 2.*

(bb) The first ection of this act was held unconstitutional in *McCracken v. Moody,* 33—81.

VIOLATION OF SCHOOL LAWS—DUTY OF PROSECUTING ATTORNEYS.

SEC. 6257. The prosecuting attorney of each judicial district shall, upon being satisfied that any violation of the school laws of this state has been committed by any officer or person, in any county of his district, which renders such officer or person so offending liable to any fine, pain, penalty or forfeiture for damage, without delay, institute in any court of competent jurisdiction such proceedings as are necessary to bring such offender to trial, and secure to the county school district, or person damaged by such violation, the benefits and reliefs to which each or any of them may be entitled ; and for such services the prosecuting attorney shall be allowed the same compensation as he is allowed in cases of misdemeanor, which shall be assessed against such offender as cost. *Act March* 11, 1881, *sec.* 10.

SPECIAL ACT FOR THE REGULATION OF PUBLIC SCHOOLS IN CITIES AND TOWNS.

SEC. 6258. Any incorporated city or town in this state, including the territory annexed thereto for school purposes, may be organized into and established as a single school district in the manner and with the powers hereinafter specified. *Act Feb.* 4, 1869, *sec.* 1.

SEC. 6259. Upon the written petition of twenty voters of such city or town, praying that the sense of the legal voters of said city or town may be taken on the adoption of this act for the regulation and government of the public schools therein, it shall be the duty of the mayor of such city or town, within five days after the presentation of such petition, to designate and fix a day, not less than seven nor more than fifteen days distant, for holding an election in said city or town for that purpose, and also for the election by ballot, at the same time, of a board of six school directors for said city or town.

SEC. 6260. The mayor shall cause notice of said election to be given by posting notices in at least five public places in said city or town, and by one insertion in such newspapers as may be published in said city or town. The electors at said election desiring to vote in favor of the adoption of this act shall have written or printed on their ballots, " For the school law," and those opposed thereto shall have written or printed on their ballots, " Against the school law ;" and, if a majority of the ballots cast at said election shall be " For school law," then, and in that case only, shall such city or town be deemed and held to be a single school district under and in pursuance of this act, and the directors voted for and elected at said election shall qualify and enter upon the discharge of their duties as hereinafter provided.

SEC. 6261. Said election shall be held at the same places and conducted in the same manner as elections for municipal officers of said city or town ; and the returns of said election shall be made to the mayor and aldermen of said city or town, who shall declare the result of said election ; and, if this act is adopted, they shall cause notice to be given to the persons elected directors.

SEC. 6262. Immediately after receiving notice of their election, and taking the oath of office required of school directors, which oath shall be filed with the clerk or recorder of said city or town, said directors shall meet, and, by lot, determine the length of time of their respective terms of office. Two shall serve until the third Saturday in December next after their election, two for one year thereafter, two for two years thereafter, and on the third Saturday in December next after the first election, and annually on that day thereafter, there shall be chosen, in the same manner, two directors, who shall serve for three years, and until their successors are elected and qualified. Said board shall fill any vacancy that may occur therein until the next annual election for directors, when such vacancy shall be filled by election. *Ib.*, sec. 2.

SEC. 6263. Said board of directors shall organize by choosing from their own number a president and secretary, who shall hold their offices until the last Saturday in December, and annually on that day said board shall meet and elect from their number a president and secretary. *Ib.*, sec. 3.

SEC. 6264. Said board of directors shall hold a regular meeting on the last Saturday in each month, and may hold stated meetings at such other times and places in said district as they may appoint ;

four members of said board shall constitute a quorum, but a less
number may adjourn from time to time; special meetings thereof
may be called by the president, or by any two members of the
board, on giving one day's notice of the time and place of the
same, and, in case of the absence of the president at any meeting of
the board, a president *pro tempore* shall be chosen. The office of
any member of said board, as such, who shall, without good cause,
fail to attend three consecutive monthly or stated meetings of said
board, may be declared vacant by the board. The board may make
rules and regulations for their own government and for the dispatch
and regulation of the school business and affairs of the district not
inconsistent with law. *Ib.*, sec. 4.

SEC. 6265. Said board of directors shall have power to purchase
or lease school-house sites, to build, hire or purchase school-houses,
and to keep in repair and furnish the same with necessary seats,
desks, furniture, fixtures and fuel, and to insure the same; to fence
the school grounds, erect out-houses, provide wells, and make all
other improvements on the school-house grounds and school-houses
belonging to the said district necessary and proper for the comfort,
convenience and health of the scholars and the preservation of said
property; to hire teachers for all public schools of the district;
employ a superintendent of the schools, who may also be principal
of any graded or high school that said board may establish; to provide books and apparatus for the schools, and the necessary blank
books and stationery for the board, and school registers and the
blanks for the teachers; to establish and maintain a sufficient number of primary, graded or high schools to accommodate all the
scholars in said district (*); to determine the branches to be taught
and the text-books to be used in the several schools of the district
(†); to admit pupils not belonging to the district on such terms as
they may agree upon with the parents or guardians of said pupils, or the
district from whence they came; to appoint a board of three visitors
and examiners for the schools of the district, which board shall examine
persons applying to teach in any of the schools in said district;

(*) But no tax for any purpose can now be levied by the county court without a vote of the
electors of the district. *Art. XIV, sec. 3. Const.; Cole v. Blackwell*, 88–271.

(†) See Sxcs. 6167, 6216.

provided, no teacher shall be employed who does not hold a certificate from the state superintendent or county examiner ; to examine, from time to time, the books and the accounts of the county treasurer, so far as the same relate to the several school funds belonging to the district; and when, in the opinion of a majority of the members of said board, the best interests of the district demand a sale or exchange of any real estate or school-house site belonging to the district, they may sell or exchange the same, the deed therefor to be executed by the president of the board upon a majority vote of the whole board of directors authorizing and directing such sale or exchange. *Ib., sec.* 5.

SEC. 6266. It shall be the duty of said board, as soon as the means for that purpose can be provided, to establish in said district an adequate number of primary schools, so located as best to accommodate the inhabitants thereof; and it shall be the further duty of said board to establish in said district a suitable number of other schools of a higher grade, wherein instruction shall be given in such studies as may not be provided for in the primary schools; the number of schools, the grades thereof, and the branches to be taught in each and all of said schools to be determined by said board. It shall be the duty of said board to keep said schools in operation not less than three nor more than ten months in each year. The said board shall have power to make and enforce all necessary rules and regulations for the government of teachers and pupils in said schools. Said board shall also, separately or collectively, together with such persons as they may appoint or invite, visit the schools in the district at least twice in each year, and observe the discipline, mode of teaching, progress of the pupils, and see that the teachers keep a correct register of the pupils, embracing the periods of time during which they attend school, the branches taught, and such other matters as may be required by law or by the instructions of the state superintendent. *Ib., sec.* 6.

SEC. 6267. No draft or warrant shall be drawn on the county treasurer, except in pursuance of an order of said board; all drafts or warrants on the treasurer shall be signed by the president, or president *pro tempore,* and the secretary, and shall specify the fund on which they are drawn and the use for which the money is assigned. *Ib., sec.* 8.

SEC. 6268. The secretary shall record all the proceedings of the board in books kept for that purpose; shall make and preserve copies of all reports required by law to be made to the state superintendent of public instruction or county examiner; shall file all papers transmitted to him pertaining to the business of the district; shall make, or cause to be made, the annual enumeration of the youth of the district in the time and manner required by law of school directors, and shall perform such other duties as the board of directors may order and direct; and for his services may be allowed reasonable compensation, to be audited and allowed by a majority of said board. The other members of said board shall receive no compensation for their services. *Ib., sec.* 9.

SEC. 6269. The title of all real estate and other property belonging, for school purposes, to any city or town organized into a separate school district under this act shall vest, and hereby is vested, in said city or town, as a school district, and shall be under the management and control of the board of school directors for said district as fully and completely as other school property belonging to said district. *Ib., sec.* 10.

SEC. 6270. All school districts formed under and governed by this act shall be known by the name of the city or town constituting the district, with the words "School District of" prefixed thereto (as, for example, "School District of Little Rock"); and, by such name, may sue and be sued, contract and be contracted with, purchase, acquire, hold and sell property, receive gifts, grants and bequests, and generally shall possess and enjoy all the corporate powers usually possessed by bodies corporate of like character. The style of the board of directors for school districts under this act shall be, "Board of School Directors." *Ib., sec.* 11.

SEC. 6271. The board of school directors of any district organized under this act shall pay and discharge all debts and liabilities lawfully incurred by the several school districts existing under previous law and embraced in the district organized under this act. *Ib., sec.* 12.

SEC. 6272. Any person elected a director under the provisions of this act who shall fail to take the oath of office and qualify as herein required, or who, after qualifying as. such director, shall fail to perform and discharge the official duties incumbent upon him as a director, shall be liable to the same penalties that now are or may be hereafter provided by law against directors of school districts for failing or refusing to qualify, or for neglect of official duty. *Ib., sec.* 13.

SEC. 6273. The board of directors may fix the term of office and define the duties of the board of visitors and examiners of the public schools in their district, and any person appointed by the board of directors a member of said board of visitors and examiners who shall refuse to act as such, and discharge the duties pertaining to such position, shall forfeit and pay to said district the sum of twenty-five dollars, to be recovered in civil action in the name of said district, and added to the teachers' fund belonging to said district. *Provided,* that no person shall be compelled to serve in that capacity more than three consecutive years. Said board of visitors and examiners shall receive no compensation for their services. *Ib., sec.* 14.

SEC. 6274. All school districts organized under this act shall have and receive their full proportion and distributive share of the general school fund of the state, in the same manner and according to the same rule as it is or may be apportioned to other districts. *Ib., sec.* 15.

SEC. 6275. It shall be the duty of the state superintendent and county examiners to make such suggestions and recommendations to the board of directors in relation to organizing and conducting the public schools in the districts organized under this act as they shall deem important.

SEC. 6276. The provisions of the general school laws of the state which are now or may hereafter be in force, when not inapplicable, and so far as the same are not inconsistent with and repugnant to the provisions of this act shall apply to districts organized under this

act; and such provisions of said laws as are inconsistent with and repugnant to the provisions of this act, and inapplicable to districts
organized thereunder, shall have no operation, force or effect in such
districts. The county court shall annex contiguous territory to
single school districts, under the provisions of this act, when a
majority of the legal voters of said territory and the board of directors of said single district shall ask, by petition, that the same shall
be done. *Ib.*, *secs.* 16, 17.

SCHOOL LANDS.

SEC. 6277. ·Whenever the inhabitants of any congressional township in this state shall desire the sale of the sixteenth section of such
township, or for any land substituted therefore, they may by written
petition, signed by a majority of the male inhabitants of such township, require the collector of taxes of the county wherein such school
land is situated to sell the same. *Act March* 22, 1881, *sec.* 1.

SEC. 6278. Upon the reception of such petition, the collector
shall ascertain that it is signed by a majority of the male inhabitants
of such township, and shall immediately proceed to divide the land
into forty-acre tracts; and after making such division, a statement
or plat of the same and number of each tract shall be made, so that
the boundaries may be defined and ascertained, which statement or
plat of the sections shall be used as a guide in advertising and selling
said lands. *Provided*, that the collector may, when necessity requires
it, call the county surveyor of his county to assist in such survey and
division; and he shall be allowed and paid, out of the interest of
the funds arising from the sale of such school lands by the said collector, such compensation as he is allowed by law for similar services; and the receipt of such surveyor to said collector shall be a
sufficient voucher for the money so paid. *Act April* 12, 1869, *sec*
4, *and act March* 22, 1881, *sec.* 2.

SEC. 6279. In subdividing shool lands for sale, no tract shall
contain more than forty acres; and the division may be made into
town or village lots, with roads, streets or alleys between them. *Ib.*,
sec. 5.

SEC. 6280. In all sales of school lands, such sales shall commence at the north-east corner tract, which shall be numbered one, and shall be made in tracts of not more than forty acres each, so long as there shall be as much as forty acres remaining to be sold. *Act July* 18, 1868, *sec.* 2.

SEC. 6281. The collector shall cause each tract or subdivision of such school land to be appraised at a fair value by three disinterested house-holders of the county, each of whom shall take an oath, which shall be indorsed upon the appraisement, that he does not desire or intend to buy said land, or any part thereof, and that he will not, directly or indirectly, be or become interested in the purchase thereof at the sale to be made by the collector. Such appraisement shall be returned to the collector.

SEC. 6282. The collector shall then give notice that he will sell the said school land at the court-house door of the county, on the first day of the next term of the county court, upon the terms prescribed by law. Such notice shall be published in some newspaper published in the county where the land is situated at least four weeks before the day of sale. If there be no newspaper published in said county, then the collector shall post up written notices in at least six of the most public places of the county four weeks before the day of sale. The collector shall also, in either case, put up a copy of the notice upon the school-house situated on the land, if there be one thereon ; if not, at the most public place on the land.

SEC. 6283. Upon the day of sale the collector shall offer the lands at public auction in separate subdivisions, beginning with number one and ending with the last mentioned division. Such sale shall be made between the hours of 12 M. and 3 P. M., but may be continued from day to day, at the same place and between the same hours, until all have been sold or offered. The sale shall be made upon the terms of one-fourth cash, the balance payable in one two and three years from date, in equal payments, bearing interest at the rate of eight per centum per annum from date of sale until paid. The purchaser shall at once pay the cash payment and execute and deliver to the collector his notes, payable to the treasurer of the county and his successors in office, for the deferred payments and interest.

SEC. 6284. If any bidder shall fail to perfect his bid, by paying the cash payment and executing his notes, the collector shall immediately re-sell the land, and the bidder shall be responsible for the difference between his bid and the price at which the land sold, which may be recovered from him by the collector in an action for the use of the township.

SEC. 6285. No tract or subdivision shall be sold for less than three-fourths of its appraised value. If any tract offered is not sold, it may be offered again, upon like notice, upon the first day of the next or any succeeding term of the county court, and be so offered until sold, without a new petition.

SEC. 6286. The purchaser shall not make merchandise of the wood on said land, or remove, or permit it to be removed or cut down, save for improvements on the land ; and the bond and security shall be given for the faithful performance of this requirement until the full amount of the purchase money is paid.

SEC. 6287. The collector shall; without delay, report all sales to the county court, which may reject or confirm the same. If any sale be rejected, the court may order the collector to again advertise and offer the land, and may specify the minimum price at which the tract may be sold, not to be less than two-thirds of appraised value. If the sale be confirmed, the collector shall execute and deliver to the purchaser a certificate in the following form :

" I, ——— ———, collector in and for the county of ——— certify that ——— ———— has purchased lot No. ——, of section ——, in township ——, range ——, for the price of ——— dollars, of which he has paid cash ———dollars, and has executed his three notes, each for ——— dollars, maturing at one, two and three years from this date, bearing interest at the rate of eight per centum per annum from date. If said notes and interest are paid at maturity, I, or my successor in office, will convey said lot of land to said ——— ——— ; but if either of said notes be not paid at maturity, said ——— ——— — shall surrender to me possession of said land, and shall forfeit his purchase and the money paid. '   A. B,
" *Collector of* ——— *County.*"

The purchaser shall thereupon be entitled to take possession of the land and to improve the same ; but if he shall fail to pay either note at maturity, he shall forfeit his purchase and all money paid.   If the sale be rejected by the county court, the collector shall return to the purchaser his notes and money.   In all cases proper orders of confirmation or rejection shall be entered of record by the court.

SEC. 6288.   Out of the cash payment the collector shall pay costs of advertising and costs of orders of confirmation or rejection of sale. He may also retain two per cent. of the cash payment for his services.   The residue of money and notes he shall deliver to the . county treasurer, who shall keep the same separate as the property of the township to which the land belongs, under direction of the county.   The treasurer shall lend all moneys belonging to township in his hands, keeping each and the security for each separate by townships, taking as security for the money loaned a note, with one responsible person as security, and a trust conveyance of real estate worth, excluding improvements, at least double the sum loaned thereon ; interest thereon to be paid annually at ten per cent. Loans may be made for five years, but on failure to pay any installment of interest, the principal shall become due, and the land taken as security shall be subject to sale for the payment thereof, whether so expressed in the deed or not.

SEC. 6289.   On the day that the apportionment of school funds is made by the county court, the treasurer shall report to the court the amount of interest in his hands belonging to each congressional township in his county, and the court shall apportion the interest so belonging to each township to and among the schools kept or taught in such townships.

SEC. 6290.   If any purchaser shall fail to pay his notes, or either of them, the treasurer or his successor in office shall at once notify the county collector of such default, and thereupon the collector shall immediately and without warrant or writ enter upon and take possession of the tract upon which default of the purchase money has been made, and shall advertise and sell the same in the same manner that the sale in the first instance was made, except that no petition for sale shall be necessary.   *Provided*, that if the purchaser shall pay the amount of the note due, all interest thereon, the cost of advertising and a fee of two per cent. of the amount due to the collector, upon or before the day of sale, the sale shall not be made, and the collector shall redeliver possession to the purchaser.

SEC. 6291. When any purchaser makes full payment of all purchase money and interest, the treasurer shall give him a certificate that full payment has been made, and, upon presentation of such certificate to the county collector for the time being, the collector shall, at the expense of the purchaser, convey the tract mentioned in the treasurer's certificate to such purchaser, his heirs and assigns.

SEC. 6292. The county treasurer shall receive for his compensation two per cent. of the interest collected, and no more. *Act March* 22, 1881, *secs.* 3–10.

SEC. 6293. As soon as practicable, the commissioner of state lands shall turn over to the county clerks of the several counties in this state all books, maps, papers, surveys and evidences of debt pertaining to the sixteenth section in the several counties, and all collectors shall pay over to the treasuries of their respective counties all funds in their hands; or that may come into their hands, arising from the sale of the sixteenth section. *Ib.*, *sec.* 11, *as amended by act March* 10, 1883.

SEC. 6294. Where the county line runs through a congressional township, the sheriff shall pay over to the county treasurers of each of the counties in which a part of such township is situated a *pro rata* share of any moneys arising from the sale of the sixteenth section, according to the number of acres in each county so interested. *Act March* 10, 1883, *sec.* 2.

PATENTS.

SEC. 6295. When the purchaser of any portion of the common school lands has heretofore assigned, or may hereafter assign, the certificate of purchase of such land, the title thereof may be made directly to the last assignee of such certificate of purchase, upon full payment of all the purchase money and interest due on said land. *Act April* 12, 1869, *sec.* 10.

SEC. 6296. If any person who shall have purchased any portion of the sections of school lands from the collector of any of the counties of this state, and paid one-fourth the purchase money therefor, and received a bond for title from such collector, shall die before such payment is fully made, and the executor, administrator, guardian or legal representative of such deceased person shall pay or cause to be paid the balance, if any, that shall be due to the collector on said purchase, upon the certificate of the collector of the proper county that the whole of the purchase money, with all the interest due thereon, has been fully paid, the auditor shall forthwith execute a deed, as is now required by law, to the heirs at law of such deceased person (‡). *Ib., sec.* 11.

SEC. 6297. The land thus conveyed to the heirs shall stand charged with the amount of money necessarily advanced to the school fund, in order to procure title, and shall, in other respects, be chargeable with the rights and incumbrances that would have attached had it descended regularly to the same heirs. *Ib.*

SEC. 6298. All patents issued for sixteenth section, or any part thereof, or common school land during the war of the rebellion, and all the official acts ot the officers of this state, in regard to such lands, during the said war, and also all deeds made by the common school commissioners of the several counties in compliance with an act of the legislature of the state, entitled, " An act to relieve certain citizens of Arkansas who purchased school lands," passed March 4,.1867, are hereby confirmed, ratified and made valid, and full faith and credit shall be given to said patents, deeds and official acts in all the courts of this state. *Provided,* nothing herein shall be construed to prevent the setting aside of any of said deeds or patents for actual fraud or mistake.

SEC. 6299. Any right, title or interest which the State of Arkansas may have acquired, or holds by virtue of any judgment, decree, execution or sale of any court in this state, in lands for which patents or deeds have been made and issued as mentioned in section 6298, is hereby vested in the proper owners thereof under such deeds or patents.

SEC. 6300. The attorney representing the State of Arkansas is hereby instructed and required to dismiss all suits now pending for

(‡) See SEC. 6301.
84

school lands where patents or deeds have been made therefor, as specified in section 6298, or if it does not appear on the face of the pleadings filed that such patents or deeds have been made, then the patent or deed may be pleaded in bar of the suit, or the court may dismiss the suit on exhibition and profert of such deed or patent; and where judgment or decree has been entered, and sale has not been made, the state's attorney shall enter satisfaction in full thereof on the presentation to him of such deed or patent.

SEC. 6301. If any purchaser of school lands shall have paid the purchase money thereof, and received no deed or patent therefor, or if any person now owing for school lands bought shall hereafter pay out his indebtedness therefor, and shall produce to the auditor satisfactory evidence of such payment, the auditor shall be, and he is hereby, authorized and required to execute to such person, or to his legal representative, a deed conveying all the right, title and interest of the State of Arkansas in such lands; but if payment has not been made before suit is begun, the purchaser shall also pay the costs of the suit. *Provided*, this act shall only apply to purchases of school lands made before the passage of this act. *Act Dec.* 14, 1875.

LEASE OF SCHOOL LANDS.

SEC. 6302. All school lands in any county in this state susceptible of cultivation shall be leased by the county collector of said county from the first to the tenth of January in each year. *Act April* 10, 1869, *sec.* 12.

SEC. 6303. The manner and terms of leasing said lands shall be by public outcry to the highest bidder, the lessee paying one-half the amount of rent in cash at the time of leasing and the balance at the end of the year. *Ib.*

SEC. 6304. At least twenty days' public notice of the time and place of offering such lands for rent or lease shall be given by said collector by publishing the same in the newspapers of the county and by posting up hand bills at the most prominent points throughout the country. *Ib.*

SEC. 6305. If any school lands offered for rent or lease at the time and in the manner above indicated shall not bring such price as the collector shall think a reasonable rent therefor, he shall be authorized to rent the same by private contract for the ensuing year, or for a longer term if he shall deem it expedient. *Ib.*

SEC. 6306. The occupants of school lands prior to the passage of this act shall be required to pay a reasonable annual rental during the time said lands have been so occupied. *Ib.*

SEC. 6307. The lessees of school lands shall be subject to the same provisions governing the lessees of other property. *Provided*, that it shall not be rented for a less amount than was offered at public sale. *Ib.*

AMENDMENTS.

SCHOOL LAWS

GENERAL ASSEMBLY of the STATE OF ARKANSAS,

SESSION 1885.

ACT XXX.

AN ACT to amend section 6283 of the Revised Statutes of Arkansas.

SECTION.
1. Amends Section 6283 of the Revised Statutes.

Be it enacted by the General Assembly of the State of Arkansas:

SECTION 1. That Section 6283 be so amended as to read as follows: Upon the day of sale the collector shall offer the lands at public auction in separate sub-divisions, beginning with number one and ending with the last mentioned division. Such sale shall be made between the hours of 12 M. and 3 P. M., but may be continued from day to day, at the same place and between the same hours, until all have been sold or offer[r]ed. The sale shall be made upon the terms of one-fourth cash, the balance payable in one, two and three years from date in equal payments, bearing interest at the rate of eight per centum per annum from date of sale until paid. The purchaser shall at once pay the cash payment and execute and deliver to the collector his notes, payable to the treasurer of the county, and his successors in office, for the deferred payments and interest, *provided*, that the purchaser may pay all such bid in cash, or may, at any time before maturity, pay off said notes with accrued interest. *Provided*, that such lands shall not be sold for less than one dollar and a quarter ($1.25) per acre.

Approved February 27th, 1885.

ACT LIII.

AN ACT to authorize the County Courts of this State to place to the credit
of the "Common School Fund" any and all school funds in the County
Treasuries, whenever there is any doubt as to the proper placing of said
funds.

PREAMBLE.

Misappropriation of County School Funds.

SECTION.

1. County Courts shall apportion to each School District its share of the School Funds of
county.
2. The principal derived from sale of 16th section shall not be apportioned.
3. All laws and parts thereof in conflict with this Act are repealed, and this Act in force
from passage.

Whereas, There exists certain school funds in the county treasury
of many of the counties of this State, derived from various sources,
about which there is some doubt with the County Courts as to their
proper application ; and

Whereas, These funds are, in many instances, deposited in banks
and used in said banks as funds for the transaction of exchange
business, and bring no interest to the School Fund, and in other
instances said school funds have lain for years in the safes of
county treasurers without any benefit accruing therefrom to the
schools of said counties; and

Whereas, It is utterly impossible for the County Courts to otherwise equitably appropriate said funds, unless relief in this direction
is granted by the Legislature, therefore

Be it enacted by the General Assembly of the State of Arkansas:

SECTION 1. That the County Courts of the various counties in
the State of Arkansas are hereby authorized and empowered to
place to the credit of the Common School Fund of the county, any
and all school funds that may be in the county treasury, derived
from various sources, and about which there is any doubt as to their
proper application with the County Court, and that said school funds,
when so placed to the credit of the Common School Fund, shall be,
by said County Courts, apportioned among the school districts of
the county as is now provided by law.

SEC. 2. The principal arising from the sale of the sixteenth
(16th) section of land shall never be apportioned or used, and should
any of the funds mentioned in this Act arise from the sale of said

sixteenth (16th) section of land and there should be any doubt as to the township from whence it came, then such townships as have not disposed of the sixteenth (16th) section of land, or may have disposed of the same and have the proceeds placed to their credit, shall not be entitled to any part of the interest arising from said doubtful sixteenth (16th) section fund.

SEC. 3. That all laws and parts of laws in conflict with this Act be, and the same are, hereby repealed, and that this Act take effect and be in force from and after its passage.

Approved March 13, 1885.

ACT LXIX.

AN ACT to amend sections six thousand two hundred and sixty-two (6262), and six thousand two hundred and sixty-three (6263), of the Revised Statutes of Arkansas.

SECTION.

1. Amends section 6262 of revised statutes relating to school directors.
2. Amends section 6263.
3. Conflicting laws repealed, and this Act in force and effect from passage.

Be it enacted by the General Assembly of the State of Arkansas:

SECTION 1. That section six thousand two hundred and sixty-two (6262) of the Revised Statutes of Arkansas, be so amended as to read as follows: Immediately after receiving notice of their election and taking the oath of office required of school directors, which oath shall be filed with the clerk or recorder of said city or town, said directors shall meet and by lot determine the length of time of their respective terms of office. Two shall serve until the third (3) Saturday in May next after their election; two for one year thereafter; two for two years thereafter, and on the third (3rd) Saturday in May next after the first election, and annually thereafter, there shall be chosen in the same manner two (2) directors, who shall serve for three years,and until their successors are elected and qualified. Said Board shall fill any vacancy that may occur therein, until the next annual election for directors, when such vacancy shall be filled by election. The ballot of the voter, in addition to the names of the persons voted for at said annual election, shall have written or printed on it the words: "For tax" or "Against tax," and the rate the voter desires levied. In other respects said annual election shall be governed by the general school law.

SEC. 2. That section six thousand two hundred and sixty-three (6263) be so amended as to read as follows: Said Board of Directors shall organize by choosing from their own number a president and secretary, who shall hold their offices until the last Saturday in May, and annually on that day said Board shall meet and elect from their number a president and secretary.

SEC. 3 That all laws and parts of laws in conflict with this Act be, and the same are, hereby repealed, and that this Act take effect and be in force from and after its passage.

Approved March 21, 1885.

ACT LXX.

AN ACT to amend sections six thousand two hundred and fifty-five (6255) and six thousand two hundred and fifty-six (6256) of the Revised Statutes of Arkansas.

SECTION.
1. Amends section 6255 of the Revised Statutes, relating to orders on the treasurer for schoo funds.
2. Amends section 6256, requiring warrants to be endorsed in case no funds to pay them.
3. Conflicting laws repealed, and this Act in force from and after passage

Be it enacted by the General Assembly of the State of Arkansas:

SECTION 1. That section six thousand two hundred and fifty-five (6255) of the Revised Statutes of Arkansas be so amended as to read as follows: The order of any board of directors, properly drawn after the passage of this Act, other than those of single school districts in cities and towns, shall be presented to the treasurer of the proper county within sixty days after it was drawn by said board of directors. All such orders shall be paid in the order of their presentation.

SEC. 2. That section six thousand two hundred and fifty-six

(6256) of the Revised Statutes of Arkansas be amended as to read as follows: If there are no funds with which to pay such order the treasurer shall endorse the same : "Not paid for want of funds," giving the date and signing his name officially. He shall number and record each warrant in the book provided for such purpose, keeping a separate record for each district, and shall pay said warrants in the order of their number.

SEC. 4. That all laws and parts of laws in conflict with this Act be, and the same are, hereby repealed, and that this Act take effect and be in force from and after its passage.

Approved March 21st, 1885.

ACT LXXXVII.

AN ACT to amend section six thousand, two hundred and thirty-six (6236), of Revised Statutes of Arkansas, eighteen hundred and eighty-four (1884).

SECTION.

1. Amends section 6236 of the Revised Statutes, relating to duties of school directors
2. Repeals conflicting laws and this Act in force from passage.

Be it enacted by the General Assembly of the State of Arkansas:

SECTION 1. That section six thousand, two hundred and thirty-six (6236), of the Revised Statutes of Arkansas, eighteen hundred and eighty-four (1884) be, and the same is, hereby amended so as to read as follows : The directors shall cause the public schools in their districts to be closed on the days appointed for public examination of teachers in their county, and also cause the said school to be closed during the session of the Teacher's Institute ; *Provided,* That said schools shall not be closed for a greater length of time than five (5) days during any one session of not more than five (5) months.

SEC. 2. That all laws and parts of laws in conflict with this Act be, and the same are, hereby repealed and this Act take effect and be in force from and after its passage.

Approved March 27th, 1885.

ACT·CIII.

AN ACT regulating the sale of the Sixteenth (16th) Sections, and to provide
for the collection of all claims due the School Fund arising from the
sales of said Sixteenth (16th) Sections and for other purposes.

SECTION.

1. Inhabitants of any Congressional township may petition for sale of sixteenth sections.
2. Duties of Collector on receipt of petition.
3. In subdividing no tract shall contain more than forty acres.
4. Collector shall cause each subdivision to be appraised.
5. Collector shall give public notice of time of sale.
6. Collector shall offer each tract for sale separately. Sale shall take place between hours of 12 m. and 3 p. m., and may be continued from day to day. No tract shall be sold for less than appraisement. If any tract remain unsold Collector may without petition sell again, giving notice of sale.
7. Collector shall report sales to the County Court.—If sales not confirmed court shall direct Collector to advertise and sell again. Form of certificate to be given purchaser. Commissioner of State Lands shall make deed on presentation of certificate.
8. Collector shall pay all costs of sales out of proceeds.
9. County c'erks shall ascertain who are paying taxes on 16th sections. Other duties.
10. County clerks shall keep the account of each township entitled to benefits from this Act.
11. Penalty imposed on county clerk for failing to keep record.
12. Authorizes Attorney-General to employ competent attorneys in each county to collect claims due on account of 16th sections. Other duties.
13. State Treasurer shall place to credit of proper county all moneys received on account 16th section lands.
14. State Treasurer to invest money and place accrued interest to credit of each county.
15. Accrued interest may be drawn in same manner as now provided for by law.
16. All evidences of indebtedness arising from sales of 16th sections shall be turned over to Commissioner of State Lands.
17. County Collectors and Treasurers shall turn over to State Treasurer all the moneys in their hands belonging to 16th section fund.
18. Commissioner of State Lands shall keep record of all deeds made for 16th section lands.
19. Conflicting laws repealed and this Act in force from passage.

Be it enacted by the General Assembly of the State of Arkansas :

SECTION 1. Whenever the inhabitants of any Congressional
township in this State shall desire the sale of the sixteenth (16th)
section of such township, or of any land substituted therefor, they
may, by written petition signed by a majority of the male inhabitants of such township require the Collector of taxes of the county
wherein such land is situated to sell the same.

SEC. 2. Upon the reception of such petition, the Collector shall ascertain that it is signed by a majority of the male inhabitants of
such township and shall immediately proceed to divide the land into
forty acre tracts, and after making such division, a statement or
plat of the same and number of each tract shall be made so that the

boundaries may be defined and ascertained, which statement or plat of the sections shall be used as a guide in advertising and selling said lands. *Provided*, that the Collector may, when necessity requires it, call the County Surveyor of his county to assist in such survey and division, and he shall be allowed and paid out of the funds arising from the sale of such school lands by said Collector such compensation as he is allowed by law for similar services, and the receipt of such Surveyor to said Collector shall be a sufficient voucher for the money so paid.

Sec. 3. In subdividing the sixteenth (16th) section lands for sale, no tract shall contain more than forty (40) acres, and the division may be made into town or city lots with roads, streets or alleys between them.

Sec. 4. The Collector shall cause each tract or subdivision of such school land to be appraised at a fair value by three (3) disinterested house-holders of the county, each of whom shall take an oath which shall be endorsed upon the appraisement that he does not desire or intend to buy said land or any part thereof and that he will not directly or indirectly be or become interested in the purchase thereof at the sale to be made by the Collector; such appraisement shall be returned to the Collector.

Sec. 5. The Collector shall then give notice that he will sell the said school lands at the Court House door of the county on the first day of the next term of the County Court upon the terms prescribed by law. Such notice shall be published in some newspaper published in the county where the land is situated at least four weeks before the day of sale. If there be no newspaper published in said county, then the Collector shall post up written notices in at least six (6) of the most public places of the county four weeks before the day of sale. The Collector shall also in either case put up a copy of the notice upon the school-house situated on the land, if there be one thereon; if not, at the most public place on the land.

Sec. 6. Upon the day of sale the Collector shall offer the lands at public auction in separate subdivisions, beginning with number one (1) and ending with the last mentioned division. Such sale shall be made between the hours of 12 M. and 3 P. M., but may be

continued from day to day at the same place and between the same
hours until all have been sold or offered. The sale shall be made
for cash. If any bidder shall fail to perfect his bid by paying the
cash, the Collector shall immediately re-sell the land and the bidder
shall be responsible for the difference between his bid and the price
at which the land sold, which may be recovered from him by the
Collector, in action for the use of the township and the Collector
shall, if necessary, at once institute suit against such bidder to recover the amount of difference between his bid and the price at
which the land sold. No tract or such division shall be sold for
less than three-fourths of its appraised value. *Provided further*,
that no tract or subdivision of the sixteenth (16) section lands shall
be sold at a less price than one dollar and twenty-five cents' ($1.25)
per acre. If any tract offered is not sold it may be offered again
upon like notice, upon the first (1st) day of the next, or any succeeding term of the County Court and so on until sold without a new
petition.

Sec. 7. The Collector shall, without delay, report all sales to the
County Court, which may reject or confirm the same. If any sale
be rejected, the County Court may direct the Collector to again
advertise and offer the land and may specify the minimum price at
which the tract or tracts may be sold, not to be less than two-thirds
($\frac{2}{3}$) of its appraised value. *Provided*, that no tract or subdivision of
the sixteenth (16th) section lands shall be sold at a less price than
one dollar and twenty-five cents ($1.25) per acre. If the sale be
confirmed by the County Court the Collector shall execute and deliver to the purchaser a certificate in the following form:

I,...... ....Collector in and for the county of............,
State of Arkansas certify that...... ....has purchased
.........of section........., in township........., range........., con-
taining.........acres, at $......... dollars per acre, and has paid to
me in full the sum of.........$.........:.. dollars. The expense of
this sale was: •

Cost of advertising, $ ....
Cost of order of confirmation, $.........
Cost of rejection of prior sale, $.........

Surveyor's fee (if any), $.........
Collector's commission, ...per cent., $...:......
Leaving a net balance of $.........
in my hands due the sixteenth (16th) section fund account of
this county.

Now, therefore, upon the presentation of this certificate to the
Commissioner of State Lands, the said...... .... , his heirs
or assigns, shall be entitled to a deed from said Commissioner
of State Lands for the tract of land above described.

....
Collector of............County.

In all cases proper orders of confirmation or rejection shall
be entered on record by the County Court.

SEC. 8. Out of the money received by the Collector for the
sale or sales of the sixteenth (16th) section lands, he shall pay
the cost of advertising, cost of confirmation order, cost of rejection of sale (if any), surveyor's fee (if any), and he may retain
for his services two (2) per cent. of the gross amount received
by him for the sale of such land ; the residue of the money received for the sale of said land, after deducting the expenses as
are above provided for, he shall at once transmit to the Treasurer of State, who shall place the amount to the credit of the
county's sixteenth (16th) section fund to which it rightfully
belongs.

SEC. 9. That the county clerks of the several counties in
this State shall examine carefully and closely the tax books of
their respective counties and ascertain what person or persons
are paying taxes on any part or parts or the whole of the sixteenth (16th) section lands, and it shall be the further duty of
the county clerks after ascertaining from the tax books the names
of any person or persons paying taxes on any of the sixteenth
(16th) section lands, and the numbers of said lands, to examine
the record of deeds and find by what authority and whether any
title or titles vest in said person or persons in whose name or
names said lands are assessed, and shall on or before the first
Monday in September, eighteen hundred and eighty-five (1885),

make and forward to the Commissioner of State Lands a full and complete statement of the exact status and condition of all of the sixteenth (16th) section lands in their respective counties. The county clerks shall be allowed the sum of forty dollars ($40.00) each for their services in making this report, and it shall be paid to them by their respective counties.

SEC. 10. That the county clerks of the several counties in this State shall keep in a well-bound book provided for that purpose, correct and accurate accounts with each and every township in their several counties, which may be entitled to any of the funds under this Act, and shall immediately after each and every sale of any part of said sixteenth (16th) sections certify to the Auditor of State the amount of moneys received by such collectors on account of such sales and the Auditor shall thereupon charge the same to such collector.

SEC. 11. That a neglect, failure or refusal, by any county clerk to perform any and all duties enjoined upon him by the provisions of this Act, shall be deemed a misdemeanor and upon conviction thereof, such clerk shall be fined in any sum not less than one hundred dollars ($100.00), nor more than five hundred dollars ($500.00), for each offense and may be removed from office.

SEC. 12. That the Attorney-General of the State of Arkansas be, and he is hereby authorized and instructed to employ competent attorneys residing in the counties in which the lands are situated to collect all claims and notes due the school fund arising from the sale of the sixteenth (16th) section lands. Before taking charge of any of such notes or claims, each of said attorneys shall be required to give bond for the faithful keeping, collecting and accounting for same, as provided for in this Act, in double the sum of the amount supposed to come into his hands, and such security as shall be approved by the Circuit Judge of the Judicial Circuit in which said attorney resides, and such bond when approved shall be filed with the Commissioner of State Lands and the Commissioner of State Lands shall, when such bond has been filed with him, turn over, or cause to be turned over to the said attorney, all notes and claims due the school fund pertaining to the sixteenth (16th) section lands. Said attorneys may retain as fees for collection, ten per cent. of the gross amount collected by them under the provisions of this Act. The remainder of said gross amount, after deducting their fees, as above provided for, shall be by said attorneys transmitted without delay to the Treasurer of State, who shall place the same to the credit of the sixteenth (16th) section fund of the county to which it rightfully belongs, and said attorneys shall prepare and forward to the Commissioner of State Lands a statement for each and every collection made by them, setting forth the name of the maker of the note or claim, the date of same, and dates of all previous payments (if any) made on such note or claim.

SEC. 13. All moneys paid into the State Treasury arising from the sale or collection of notes and claims pertaining to the sixteenth (16th) section lands, shall be by the State Treasurer placed to the credit of the county's sixteenth (16th) section fund, to which said moneys may rightfully belong, and the Treasurer of State shall, for each payment to him on account of the sixteenth (16th) section fund, issue triplicate receipts, one of which receipts shall be filed with the Auditor of State, one filed with the Commissioner of State Lands and one given to the party making the payment.

SEC. 14. The Treasurer of State shall, by, and under direction of the Board of Commissioners of the Common School Fund, as soon as practicable after the receipt of any moneys paid into the State Treasury on account of the sixteenth (16th) section fund, invest the same in either United States bonds or bonds of the State of Arkansas, and as interest accrues on said investment, he shall collect the same and place to the credit of the respective counties' sixteenth section fund accounts such interest on said investment, in the proportion to which each county is properly entitled.

SEC. 15. That the interest, accruing to the several counties and townships, that may hereafter be in the State Treasury, shall be drawn out of the Treasury in the same manner as now provided by law for drawing other funds due counties, and when drawn shall be accounted for by the County Treasurer in the same manner as for other county funds thus drawn, and the County Court shall distribute and set apart to the proper townships all such sums and funds as shall be due such township, either from the sales of sixteenth (16th) sections in such townships, or from collections of notes belonging thereto.

SEC. 16. That all notes, claims, bonds, papers or evidences of debt belonging to the school fund, arising from the sale or sales of the sixteenth (16th) section lands, in the hands of County Collectors or other persons, shall be, within ninety days after the passage of this Act, turned over to the Commissioner of State Lands.

SEC. 17. That all County Treasurers, Collectors or other persons having in their possession any funds arising from the sale or sales of the sixteenth (16th) section lands, shall within ninety days after the passage of this Act, pay the same into the State Treasury, and the State Treasurer shall place the same to the credit of the respective counties' sixteenth (16th) section fund accounts to which said funds do rightfully belong.

SEC. 18. That upon the presentation to the Commissioner of State Lands of any certificate of purchase as specified in section seven (7) of this Act, the Commissioner shall execute to the purchaser a deed for the lands therein described, and shall keep a full and complete record of all such sales and of the deeds so issued, and it shall be the further duty of the Commissioner of State Lands to keep as correct records of sale or sales of the sixteenth (16th) section lands as the reports made to him from time to time may enable him to do.

SEC. 19. That all Acts and parts of Acts in conflict with this Act be, and the same are hereby repealed, and this Act to take effect and be in force from and after its passage.

Approved March 31, 1885.
S5

APPENDIX.

APPENDIX.

Forms for the Use of School Officers.

FORM I.—FORM OF NOTICE OF MEETING FOR THE EXAMINATION OF SCHOOL TEACHERS.

Notice is hereby given that there will be a Public Examination of Teachers, at ....
the .... days of .... A. D. 18..., to ascertain the Professional Qualifications of
all persons desiring to teach in the Public Schools of .... County.

....

County Examiner.

.... County, Arkansas.

FORM II.—DIRECTORS OATH.

I, ... do solemnly swear (or affirm) that I will support the Constitution of the United States, and the Constitution of the State of Arkansas, and that I will faithfully
discharge the duties of the office of .... upon which I am now about to enter.

Sworn and subscribed to before me, this .... day of .... 18.........

....

County Clerk.

Remarks.—This Oath must be taken and subscribed before some competent officer or old director, within ten (10) days after the fifteenth (15th) of October, and filed in the office of the County
Clerk.

FORM III.—ANNUAL REPORT,

Of the Directors of District No. ...., to the County Examiner of ....
County, State of Arkansas, for the School Year ending June 30, 18....

PUPILS.

Number of White Pupils, between six and twenty-one years of age, enrolled in the Public Schools during the year; Males .... ; Females .... ; Total ....

Number of Colored Pupils, between six and twenty-one years of age, enrolled in the Public Schools during the year; Males .... ; Females .... ; Total ....

Total Number enrolled, both White and Colored : Males .... ; Females .... Total ....

Average Number of each sex in daily attendance ; Males................... .....Females......... .... ; Total ....

Total Number studying Orthography .... ; Reading .... ; Mental Arithmetic ... . ; Written Arithmetic .... ; English Grammar........................ Geography .... ; History..................... ; Higher Branches ....

TEACHERS.

.... Grade Certificate, salary $..............................per month

.... Grade Certificate, salary $......................... ......per month ;

.... Grade Certificate, salary $...........................per month ;

.... Grade Certificate, salary $...........................per month ;

Who e amount paid Teachers during the year, $.....................

Number of visits received from the Directors during the first term .... ; during the second term..........................

Number of days the school was taught by a licensed teacher ....

SCHOOL-HOUSES ERECTED DURING THE YEAR.

No. of Log .... ; Condition .... ; Cost $...................... ; No. of Frame .... ; Condition .... ; Cost $...................... ; No. of Brick .... ; Condition .... ; Cost $....................... ; No. of Stone ....; Condition .... ; Cost $....................... No. of School-Houses previously erected ; Log .... ; Frame .... ; Brick .... ; Stone .... ; Condition .... ; Value $........................

Value of all Other Property belonging to the District, $ .... ; Condition of School-House Grounds .... ; No. enclosed .... ; No. not enclosed ....

TAXES VOTED BY THE DISTRICT.

For Salaries of Teachers $........... .... ; For Purchase or Lease of Sites .... ; For Purchase, Erection or Hire of Houses ....; For Repair of Houses and Grounds .... ; For Fuel and Incidental Expenses ....; For Furniture, Apparatus, Lights, etc., ... ; For Other Purposes ....; Total Amount of Taxes Voted for ....

FINANCIAL STATEMENT.

Receipts : From State Apportionment $...................... ; From District Tax .... ; From Grants and Gifts .... ; From Sale or Lease of Houses or Sites .... From Other Sources ....; Total ....

Disbursements : Amounts drawn from County Treasury ; For Salaries of Teachers $................... ; For Purchase or Lease of Sites .... ; For Purchase, Erection or Hire of Houses .... : For Repair of Houses or Grounds ....; For Fuel and Incidental Expenses .... ; For Other Expenses ....; Total Amount drawn from County Treasury during the year ....

Revenues Remaining on Hand, subject to the order of the District ; Of State Apportionment $............. .... ; of District Tax .... ; of Grants and Gifts .... ; of Revenues derived from Sale or Lease of Houses or Sites ....; of Revenues derived from Other Sources .... ; Total Amount remaining in the County Treasury, subject to the order of the District ....

STATE OF ARKANSAS, }

County of............................} *ss.* We, ...

Directors of School District No........... ...., County of................................., being duly sworn, state on oath that the foregoing report is in all respects a just and true statement of the statistics, affairs and transactions in said District, for the time and as to the matters therein mentioned, according to the best of our knowledge and belief. So help us God.

....

....

....

Directors.

Subscrib. d and sworn to before me, this.....................day of.......................................18......

....J. P.

———

REMARKS.

....

....

Remarks. —The Board of Directors will transmit this blank properly filled out, to the County Examiner of their county, between the first and tenth days of September.

A failure to do so will subject them to the liability of a fine of twenty-five dollars ($25.00), to be recovered by action against them, at the instance of the prosecuting attorney of his district.

———————————

FORM IV.—ENUMERATION REPORT.

———

THE NAMES, AGES, SEX AND COLOR, of all persons residing in District No.................., in the County of............................., between the ages of six and twenty-one years; on the first day of September, 188..., are truly set forth in the following schedule:

No.	NAMES.	WHITE.			No.	NAMES.	COLORED.		
		Age.	Male.	Female.			Age.	Male.	Female.

ENUMERATION REPORT.— Concluded.

Deaf, Blind, Insane and Dumb.

No. Insane.	No. Deaf.	No. Blind.	No. Dumb.	Total.	NAMES.	Age.	POST-OFFICE.

Total Number White Males..... ....
Total Number White Females.............................. ....
     Aggregate ....
Total Number Colored Males.................................... ....
Total Number Colored Females.......................... ....
     Aggregate ....
Total Aggregate... ....

STATE OF ARKANSAS, }
County of... }
We,..
Directors of School District No...................., County of...................................., being duly sworn,
state on oath that the foregoing report is in all respects a just and true statement of the statistics,
affairs and transactions in said district, for the time and as to the matters therein mentioned, according to the best of our knowledge and belief. So help us God.

....
....
....
Directors.
Subscribed and sworn before me this.................... day of................................18......
.... J. P.

Remarks.—Directors will prepare this report between the first and tenth days of September,
and copy it into their record book. A failure to do so will subject them to a fine of twenty-five dollars
($25.00), and render them liable to the damages which their district may incur through their neg-
lect. (See section seventy-four of the School Law.) "Thirteenth" in the seventeenth section of
some copies of the Law, should be "Thirtieth."

FORM V.—TEACHER'S CONTRACT.
ARKANSAS.

THIS AGREEMENT, Between...
....
as Directors of District No........................., in the County of.................. ...., State of
Arkansas, and...
who agree to teach a Common School in said District, is as follows :

The said Directors agree, upon their part, in consideration of the covenants of said Teacher
hereinafter contained to employ the said... ....
to teach a Common School in said District, for the term of........ ....months,
commencing on the..........................day of.., A. D. 18......, to pay therefor in
the manner, and out of the funds provided by law, the sum of...................................dollars, for each
school month.

Said Directors further agree, that all the steps required or allowed by law to be taken by said
District and its officers, to secure the payment of teachers' wages, shall be so had and taken
promptly, and the requirements of the law, in favor of the Teacher complied with by said District.

The Teacher, on...................part, agrees to keep....... ....school open...............hours each
school day; keep carefully the Register required by law; preserve from injury to the utmost of
......................power, the District property; give said school...................entire time, and best efforts
during school-hours; use .... utmost influence with parents to secure a full attendance of
*cholars, and generally to comply with all the requirements of the laws of this State in relation to
Teachers, to the best of...............ability.

Signatures,
....
....
....
Directors.
....
Teacher.
Date, ...18......
Place, ...

Remarks.—A duplicate should be made out and given to the teacher.
No Board should allow a teacher to commence school until a contract be properly signed by
both parties. The Board should require the certificate to be presented when the contract is signed.

No..............................   *FORM VI.*   Grade No.........................

DEPARTMENT OF PUBLIC INSTRUCTION.

State of Arkansas.

TEACHER'S LICENSE.

THIS IS TO CERTIFY, That ....
having presented satisfactory testimonials of good moral character, has this day been examined in
Orthography, Reading, Writing, Mental and Written Arihmetic, English Grammar, Modern Geography, History of the United States, and is hereby LICENSED to teach the same in the Public
Schools of this State, within the limits of .... County, for the term of ....
year .... months from the date hereof, unless sooner revoked.

Given under my Hand, this .... day of .... A. D. 188......

....
County Examiner.

———

STANDING.

100 being taken as the Standard of Perfection.

Orthography .... Writing .... Mental Arithmetic ....

Modern Geography .... Reading .... English Grammar ....

Written Arithmetic .... History of the United States ....

———

FORM VII.—CERTIFICATE OF SCHOOL TAX LEVIED.

Arkansas.

Office of School Directors, District No...... ....

....18......

To the Honorable County Court of .... County, State of Arkansas.

We hereby certify, that at a Meeting of the Voters of School District No.................. to ....
County, he d on the .... day of .... 18......), it was Voted that the sum of
.... dollars be levied on the taxable property in said District, for the following School
purposes, to-wit :

Expenses of Teachers, - - -	$................ ....
Purchase or lease of site, - - -	$...
Purchase, erection or hire of site, -	$..............................
Repair of house or grounds, - - -	$.................................
Fuel, - - - - - - -	$....................................
Furniture, - . - - - - -	$...... ....
Other Purposes,	$ ....
	$............... ....
Total amount, - - - -	$...............................

And your Honorable Body will please levy a tax on the taxable property of this District, sufficient to raise the above amount, in accordance to law.

Attest :

.... Signed,
Chairman.

{ ....
....
....

Directors.

Dated this .... day of .... 18...

Remarks :—This certificate must be filed with the County Clerk on or before the first day of
October in each year.

FORM VIII.—DIRECTOR'S ESTIMATE OF DISTRICT EXPENSES.

———

ELECTORS OF SCHOOL DISTRICT NO ...., County of ...., State of Arkansas.

We respectfully submit the following as our estimate of the expenses of the Public Schools in this District, for the term of three months during the present scholastic year, beginning the first of last July, and of the expense per month of continuing the schools longer than three months :

AMOUNT NECESSARY

For Teachers' Salaries, - - - - ....

For Purchase or Lease of Sites, - - - - ....

For Purchase, Erection or Hire of Houses, - - - ....

For Repair of Houses or Grounds, - - - ....

For Fuel and Incidental Expenses, - - - - ....

For Furniture, Apparatus, Lights, etc., - - - ....

For Other Purposes, - - - - - - ....

Total, - - - - - - ══════════════

Amount which we will probably receive from State Apportionment, - - - - - - ....

Remainder to be raised by a District Tax, - - - ══════════════

Expense of continuing the Schools .... longer than Three Months at .... Dollars per Month, - - - ....

Total Amount to be raised by District Tax, - - ══════════════

The above estimate is respectfully submitted to your consideration and action.

....⎫
....⎬ Directors.
....⎭

Dated, May .... 18......

———

FORM IX.—OFFICE OF COUNTY EXAMINER.

———

.. ..County, ...18......

Board of Directors, District No.....................

You will notify all Teachers holding certificates of qualification to teach in Public Schools, that a Teachers' Institute will be held at .... on the ....days of ......,........................ 18......

Also, that Sec. 82 of the School Law requires their attendance.

Urge upon them the importance of attending.

.... County Examiner.

———

Remarks :—The importance of the TEACHERS' INSTITUTE is recognized by all leading Educators. Teachers who expect to be effective, and who aspire to an honorable place in public favor and confidence, should miss no opportunity to equip themselves for their work. Directors are requested to urge upon Teachers the duty of attending,

S6

FORM X.—COUNTY TREASURER'S FINANCIAL STATEMENT.

Of the School Revenues of..............County, for the year ending June 30, 18......

AMOUNT RECEIVED.						AMOUNT EXPENDED.					BALANCE UNEXPENDED.			
Common School Fund.	District Tax.	Sale or Lease of House or Site.	Grants or Gifts.	Other Sources.	Total.	Teachers' Salaries.	Purchasing house or site.	Building and Repairing.	Other Purposes.	Total.	Teachers' Salaries.	Building and Repairing.	Other Purposes.	Total.

..................................State Superintendent Public Instruction,
Little Rock, Ark.,

Dear Sir :

Herewith please find Statement of the School Revenues of.................................County, for the year ending June 30, 18......, as shown by the books in this office

Respectfully,

..............................., County Treasurer.

FORM XI.—DIRECTORS' WARRANT.

No............................District School Fund, District No..

Treasurer of....................................County, Arkansas :

Pay to..., or order,

the sum of..

For..out of

the ....Fund.

....

....

....

Directors.

FORM XII.—ANNUAL SCHOOL MEETING.

NOTICE.

There will be an Annual School Meeting of the Electors of School District No.........................
....County, at...
the third Saturday in May, 18...... At this meeting the following matters will be submitted to the consideration and action of the Electors of said District :

....
....

It is desired that every Elector be present.

....

....

....

Directors.

Date, ..., 18......

Directors will please bear in mind that this notice must be posted in three or more conspicuous places, at least fifteen days before the time of meeting ; and that the objects of this meeting must be inserted in the appropriate blanks above, as provided for in section 69 of the present School Law of Arkansas.

www.ingramcontent.com/pod-product-compliance
Lightning Source LLC
Chambersburg PA
CBHW020234090426
42735CB00010B/1693